BLACK&DECKER®

THE HANDY GUIDE TO
HOME
PLUMBING

CRESTLINE

Contents

Planning & Installing New Plumbing

This edition published in 2011 by CRESTLINE
a division of BOOK SALES, INC.
276 Fifth Avenue Suite 206
New York, New York 10001
USA

This edition published by arrangement with Creative Publishing
International, Inc.

Copyright © 2005
Creative Publishing international, Inc.
400 First Avenue North, Suite 300
Minneapolis, MN 55401
1-800-328-0590
www.creativepub.com
All right reserved

Printed in China
10 9 8 7 6 5 4 3 2 1

THE COMPLETE GUIDE TO HOME PLUMBING
Created by: The Editors of Creative Publishing international, Inc.,
in cooperation with Black & Decker. Black & Decker® is a trademark
of The Black & Decker Corporation and is used under license.

Library of Congress
Cataloging-in-Publication Data

The complete guide to home plumbing.--
Newly expanded 3rd ed.
    p. cm.
  Includes index.
  At head of title: Black & Decker.
  ISBN-13: 978-0-7858-2772-6
  ISBN-10: 0-7858-2772-2
  1. Plumbing--Amateurs' manuals. 2.
Dwellings--Remodeling--Amateurs'
manuals. I. Title: Home plumbing. II. Black
& Decker Corporation
(Towson, Md.) III. Creative Publishing In-
ternational.
  TH6124.C66 2005
  696'.1--dc22

Introduction

The Handy Guide to Home Plumbing is a comprehensive yet easy-to-follow plumbing manual for today's homeowner. It gives you all the practical information and know-how you need to understand, install, repair, replace, and maintain your home plumbing system with confidence.

This edition complies with current uniform plumbing and building codes. There have been significant changes in the rules governing what is and is not allowed in home plumbing. And the changes have been good news for homeowners. In *The Handy Guide to Home Plumbing*, you'll find several new projects and processes that were barely on the radar just a couple of years ago. Today, however, they're fully endorsed and offer brand-new options to make your home plumbing projects easier and less expensive.

If you've always wanted a second bathroom in the basement but didn't want to break up the concrete floor, you'll want to know about the all-new macerating toilets. If you've ever wished for supply pipe that can be bent like a garden hose but is as durable as copper, you'll want to get the scoop on PEX. From water heaters with no tank to island sinks with no complicated venting and kitchen faucets that fill pots right on the stovetop, it's all new and it's all here, in the latest edition of *The Handy Guide to Home Plumbing*.

Though most of the projects in this book are simple, many of the complex projects, such as plumbing a kitchen, also require the use of basic carpentry and electrical techniques. Before starting a project, read through the directions carefully to determine if you are prepared to complete the project with the equipment and knowledge you have, or whether you require the help of a professional plumber.

Using this Book

This book is arranged into five easy-to-follow sections. Each section contains clear directions, expert advice from professional plumbers, cross-reference charts, and hundreds of detailed color photographs to walk you through each step of any plumbing project.

The first section is an introduction to the entire plumbing system, with a glossary of common plumbing terms. You'll find an overview of the water cycle, from the distribution of fresh water to the recycling of waste water, to aid in your understanding of basic plumbing principles. Detailed models of an entire home plumbing system are also included, which contain thorough descriptions of each part of the plumbing system (with color-coded pipes for easy identification of supply and drain lines) to help you diagnose problems and plan possible repairs.

The next section illustrates how to properly plan your plumbing project. You will learn how to map out your existing plumbing system to effectively plan repairs or new installations. The reference charts provided help illustrate how to inspect and map your existing plumbing system. This section also discusses the principles that make your plumbing system work and explains how to ensure your project will comply with plumbing codes. The section ends with instructions for testing your newly installed plumbing pipes in preparation for the final inspection.

Section three shows what you will need and gives you the basic knowledge to begin and complete a plumbing project successfully. It includes photographs and descriptions of the common hand tools, specialty plumbing tools, power tools, and rental tools used in this book. This section also shows the many different kinds of pipes and fittings available, and how to cut, fit, repair, and replace each kind. The step-by-step methods illustrating how to solder copper pipes, solvent-glue plastic pipes, make mechanical unions with PEX, and replace cast-iron pipe make these once-intimidating tasks easy to understand and simple to complete.

The fourth section describes the process for adding new supply lines and waste drains and includes over a dozen common home plumbing projects. Some of these projects—particularly installing showers, tubs, sinks, whirl-pools, and dishwashers—require carpentry skills. Some projects also involve electrical work. You should be familiar with these skills before taking on any of these projects. This section also includes segments on water softeners, whole-house humidifiers, and outdoor plumbing.

Many home plumbing projects involve existing plumbing lines and fixtures instead of new ones. The fifth section of this book will help you decide whether to fix what you have, change parts of it, or tear out the old and start over. Included are directions for running new plumbing pipes when walls and floors are finished, and for replacing plumbing pipes between your water meter and individual fixtures. It also provides instructions for repairing faucets, fixing toilets, maintaining drains, fixing tub and shower plumbing, and repairing or replacing both electric and gas water heaters, including tankless models. At the conclusion of this section, you will find new maintenance information that will help lengthen the life of your water softener, water pump, and septic systems, as well as advice on how to prevent or repair some of the most common plumbing annoyances: burst, frozen, or noisy pipes.

The Handy Guide to Home Plumbing takes the mystery out of your plumbing system and its individual parts. Full of thorough instructions and helpful tips, this comprehensive reference book will be an important addition to your home improvement library.

Glossary of Terms

Access panel:
Opening in a wall or ceiling that provides access to the plumbing system

Air admittance valve:
A valve that allows air into a drain line in order to facilitate proper draining. Often used where traditional vent pipe would be difficult to install.

Appliance:
Powered device that uses water, such as a water heater, dishwasher, washing machine, whirlpool, or water softener

Auger:
Flexible tool used for clearing obstructions in drain lines

Ballcock:
Valve that controls the water supply entering a toilet tank

Blow bag:
Expanding rubber device that attaches to a garden hose; used for clearing floor drains

Branch drain line:
Pipe that connects additional lines to a drain system

Branch line:
Pipe that connects additional lines to a water supply system

Cleanout:
Cover in a waste pipe or trap that provides access for cleaning

Closet auger:
Flexible rod used to clear obstructions in toilets

Closet bend:
Curved fitting that fits between a closet flange and a toilet drain

Closet flange:
Ring at the opening of a toilet drain, used as the base for a toilet

Coupling:
Fitting that connects two pieces of pipe

DWV:
Drain, waste, and vent; the system for removing water from a house

DWV stack:
Pipe that connects house drain system to a sewer line at the bottom and vents air to outside of house at the top

Elbow:
Angled fitting that changes the direction of a pipe

Fixture:
Device that uses water, such as a sink, tub, shower, sillcock, or toilet

Flapper (tank ball):
Rubber seal that controls the flow of water from a toilet tank to a toilet bowl

Flux (soldering paste):
Paste applied to metal joints before soldering to increase joint strength

Hand auger (snake):
Hand tool with flexible shaft, used for clearing clogs in drain lines

Hose bib:
Any faucet spout that is threaded to accept a hose

I.D.:
Inside diameter; plumbing pipes are classified by I.D.

Loop vent:
A special type of vent configuration used in kitchen sink island installations

Main shutoff valve:
Valve that controls water supply to an entire house; usually next to the water meter

Motorized auger:
Power tool with flexible shaft, used for clearing tree roots from sewer lines

Nipple:
Pipe with threaded ends

O.D.:
Outside diameter

Plumber's putty:
A soft material used for sealing joints between fixtures and supply or drain parts

Reducer:
A fitting that connects pipes of different sizes

Riser:
Assembly of water supply fittings and pipes that distributes water upward

Run:
Assembly of pipes that extends from water supply to fixture, or from drain to stack

Saddle valve:
Fitting clamped to copper supply pipe, with hollow spike that punctures the pipe to divert water to another device, usually a dishwasher or refrigerator icemaker

Sanitary fitting:
Fitting that joins DWV pipes; allows solid material to pass through without clogging

Shutoff valve:
Valve that controls the water supply for one fixture or appliance

Sillcock:
Compression faucet used on the outside of a house

Soil stack:
Main vertical drain line, which carries waste from all branch drains to a sewer line

Solder:
Metal alloy used for permanently joining metal (usually copper) pipes

T-fitting:
Fitting shaped like the letter T used for creating or joining branch lines

Trap:
Curved section of drain, filled with standing water, that prevents sewer gases from entering a house

Union:
Fitting that joins two sections of pipe but can be disconnected without cutting

Vacuum breaker:
Attachment for outdoor and below-ground fixtures that prevents waste water from entering supply lines if water supply pressure drops

Wet vent:
Pipe that serves as a drain for one fixture and as a vent for another

Y-fitting:
Fitting shaped like the letter Y used for creating or joining branch lines

In a basic plumbing cycle, which is still used in many rural homes, a well pumps fresh water from the water table. A system of in-house plumbing pipes then distributes the water to various fixtures throughout the house. After use, the waste water travels through a system of drain pipes to a septic system, which separates solid wastes and returns the water to the soil. In metropolitan areas, the methods for supplying fresh water and handling waste water are more complex (see pages 10 to 11).

Understanding the Water Cycle

Each day in the United States, roughly 500 billion gallons of water are withdrawn from surface and underground water supply sources for use in homes and businesses. In private homes, water is used for drinking and food preparation, for cleaning and washing, and for irrigating landscapes and gardens. Finally, we depend on water to carry septic wastes safely away from our homes.

Just as fresh water is essential to basic human existence, a well-designed plumbing system is essential to a healthy life and productive society. The science of transporting water to and from a home through a system of pipes originated some 5,000 years ago in ancient Sumer and is still evolving today.

Most homeowners are familiar with the in-home portion of the water cycle—the plumbing system with its network of faucets, toilets, and other plumbing fixtures. Many homeowners can make minor repairs to the fixtures and pipes. However, few homeowners fully understand the beginning and ending stages of this sequence—called the hydrologic cycle. Knowing where the fresh water supply originates can help you make decisions on how to manage the water entering your home; and understanding how waste water is recycled may change your decisions on what materials to flush down the drain.

Distributing fresh water. The fresh water that enters your home originates in one of two sources: surface water or groundwater. Surface water supplies include lakes, streams, rivers, and artificial storage reservoirs. Groundwater comes from natural underground caverns or from aquifers—porous, water-saturated layers of gravel, sand, and silt. This water is either pumped from the ground through a well or rises to the surface through natural springs.

In about 25% of homes, mostly rural residences, a well delivers fresh water directly from groundwater sources with no chemical treatment. This is done because groundwater is generally regarded as pure enough to drink. In recent years, however, it has been found that some groundwater supplies have unhealthy levels of natural substances, such as nitrates, as well as toxic pollutants and dangerous microorganisms. If your water supply comes from a well, it is a good idea to have a sample tested by a laboratory. If a test finds that your water supply has harmful contaminants, consider installing an in-home purification or filtration system.

In addition, groundwater pumped from a well often has a high mineral content. This "hard" water may prematurely age your plumbing pipes, as the minerals build up on the inside surfaces of the pipes. Installing a water softener helps reduce mineral levels and can extend the life of your plumbing system.

In metropolitan areas and many smaller communities, fresh water distribution is a function of public utility. The water pumped from the ground or taken from surface sources is first cleansed at a central treatment plant before it is distributed to homes. Public utilities generally do an adequate job of purifying the water supply, but in large industrial areas, especially those that derive their water supply from surface water, it is not uncommon for very low levels of potentially harmful substances to be present. Your local division of the Environmental Protection Agency (EPA) should have information on the water quality in your area.

Recycling waste water. About 78% of all water that enters a home or business eventually finds its way back to a groundwater or surface water source. Because this waste water eventually becomes part of the fresh water supply again, it must be purified before it is released into the environment.

In rural areas, this purification is accomplished by simple home septic systems that separate solid wastes and transport the water back into the soil. As this water makes its slow journey back to the water table, it is filtered pure by many layers of rock and soil.

In most cities and towns, waste water purification is accomplished by a system of sewer utility pipes that carry raw sewage to a central treatment facility. After solid wastes are removed, the water is purified and released.

Keep in mind that individual septic systems and urban sewage treatment plants are designed to recycle waste water and organic solids only. Flushing any synthetic materials or chemicals down your drain can jeopardize the system's function to transform waste liquid into pure fresh water for the next user.

Reservoirs created by constructing dams across river valleys are common in arid western regions. By capturing water from melting snow in the mountains, communities can store enough water to supply their needs through the dry summer months. In other regions, rivers and lakes provide ongoing sources of fresh water. Many reservoirs are hydroelectric projects used to generate electricity, as well as to store fresh water.

Water towers and enclosed tanks store the water pumped from treatment plants. They are usually positioned on high ground, so gravity can produce the downward pressure necessary to force water through the water mains. Every 2.3 feet of height produces 1 pound of water pressure.

Distributing Fresh Water

Although the specific methods for collecting, treating, and distributing fresh water vary from community to community, the process is generally the same no matter where you live. Water is pumped from an underground source or is channeled from a lake, river, or reservoir into a large controlled storage facility.

From the storage reservoir, the water is pumped to a water treatment plant, where it is cleansed and purified. Water treatment plants use a variety of physical and chemical procedures. In a typical plant, water is strained and filtered to remove solids, is aerated with sprayers to remove

dissolved gases, and is then disinfected with chlorine to kill organisms. In most communities, fluoride is added to the water supply to help reduce tooth decay.

Finally, the treated fresh water is pumped to enclosed storage towers or tanks, where a network of distribution pipes carries the water to homes and businesses in the community.

Recycling Waste Water

The systems used to purify waste water after it leaves the home range from simple home septic tanks to enormous sewage treatment plants that handle millions of gallons of raw sewage each day. But no matter what system is used, the process of cleansing waste water is simple in principle.

All waste treatment systems use a combination of physical, biological, and chemical processes to remove contaminants from water. However, the success of any waste water treatment system can be compromised by improper use. Bleaches, fertilizers, and phosphorus detergents flushed into the waste system may interfere with the natural consumption of solid wastes by microorganisms. And pesticides and other chemicals poured down sink drains by homeowners may eventually find their way to the fresh water supply.

Lagoon systems are growing in popularity, especially for small communities. Originally, this design was used simply to hold untreated waste water until it evaporated, but modern lagoons are state-of-the-art treatment facilities in which aquatic plants are used to break down solid wastes. The plant material is periodically harvested and dried to create fertilizer, and the water is used to irrigate farming lands or urban landscapes.

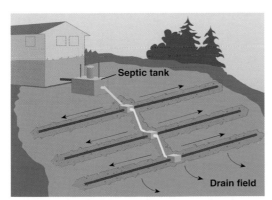

Private septic systems consist of an underground tank and a system of pipes fanning out from the tank. When sewage reaches the tank, the solid wastes settle to the bottom, where they are consumed by microorganisms. As the tank fills, the water flows out of the tank through porous drain pipes that distribute the water into the soil. The water is filtered clean as it drains down through thick layers of soil and rock on its return to the water table. Used correctly, a septic system requires only that residual solid wastes be pumped out every few years.

Sewage treatment plants are the popular urban solution for treating billions of gallons of waste water that drain from our homes and businesses. Sewage, a combination of water and solid wastes, is first directed to settling tanks, where the solid wastes precipitate to the bottom. This is followed by a biological treatment, in which microorganisms digest remaining organic material in the water. The water is then filtered, disinfected with chlorine, and discharged to irrigation canals, streams, or lakes. The residual solid waste is often processed as agricultural fertilizer.

The Home Plumbing System

Because most of a plumbing system is hidden inside walls and floors, it may seem to be a complex maze of pipes and fittings. In fact, home plumbing is simple and straightforward. Understanding how home plumbing works is an important first step toward doing routine maintenance and money-saving repairs.

A typical home plumbing system includes three basic parts: a water supply system, a fixture and appliance set, and a drain system. These three parts can be seen clearly in the photograph of the cut-away house on the opposite page.

Fresh water enters a home through a main supply line (1). This fresh water source is provided by either a municipal water company or a private underground well. If the source is a municipal supplier, the water passes through a meter (2) that registers the amount of water used. A family of four uses about 400 gallons of water each day.

Immediately after the main supply enters the house, a branch line splits off (3) and is joined to a water heater (4). From the water heater, a hot water line runs parallel to the cold water line to bring the water supply to fixtures and appliances throughout the house. Fixtures include sinks, bathtubs, showers, and laundry tubs. Appliances include water heaters, dishwashers, clothes washers, and water

softeners. Toilets and exterior sillcocks are examples of fixtures that require only a cold water line.

The water supply to fixtures and appliances is controlled with faucets and valves. Faucets and valves have moving parts and seals that eventually may wear out or break, but they are easily repaired or replaced.

Waste water then enters the drain system. It first must flow past a trap (5), a U-shaped piece of pipe that holds standing water and prevents sewer gases from entering the home. Every fixture must have a drain trap.

The drain system works entirely by gravity, allowing waste water to flow downhill through a series of large-diameter pipes. These drain pipes are attached to a system of vent pipes. Vent pipes (6) bring fresh air to the drain system, preventing suction that would slow or stop drain water from flowing freely. Vent pipes usually exit the house at a roof vent (7).

All waste water eventually reaches a main waste and vent stack (8). The main stack curves to become a sewer line (9) that exits the house near the foundation. In a municipal system, this sewer line joins a main sewer line located near the street. Where sewer service is not available, waste water empties into a septic system.

Water meter and main shutoff valves are located where the main water supply pipe enters the house. The water meter is the property of your local municipal water company. If the water meter leaks, or if you suspect it is not functioning properly, call your water company for repairs.

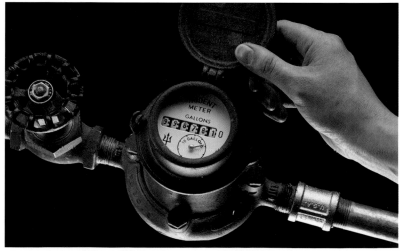

(7)
Roof vent

(8)
**Waste and
vent stack**

(6)
Vent pipe

(5)
Trap

Branch drain line

(4)
**Water
heater**

(3)
**Branch
line**

**Main
shutoff
valve**

(2)
Water meter

**Floor
drain**

Hot water
supply lines

Cold water
supply lines

Drain
lines

Vent
lines

(1) **Main supply line**

(9)
Sewer line

Water Supply System

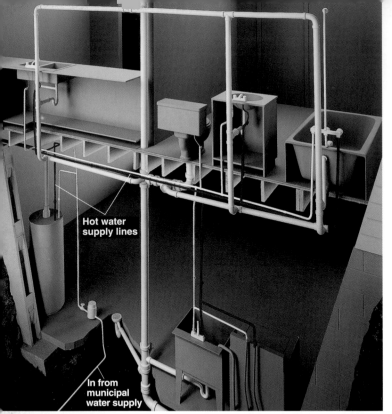

Hot water supply lines

In from municipal water supply

Cold water supply lines

Water supply pipes carry hot and cold water throughout a house. In homes built before 1960, the original supply pipes are usually made of galvanized iron. Newer homes have supply pipes made of copper. In most areas of the country, supply pipes made of rigid plastic or PEX are accepted by local plumbing codes.

Water supply pipes are made to withstand the high pressures of the water supply system. They have small diameters, usually ½" to 1", and are joined with strong, watertight fittings. The hot and cold lines run in tandem to all parts of the house. Usually, the supply pipes run inside wall cavities or are strapped to the undersides of floor joists.

Hot and cold water supply pipes are connected to fixtures or appliances. Fixtures include sinks, tubs, and showers. Some fixtures, such as toilets or hose bibs, are supplied only by cold water. Appliances include dishwashers and clothes washers. A refrigerator icemaker uses only cold water. Tradition says that hot water supply pipes and faucet handles are found on the left-hand side of a fixture, with cold water on the right.

Because it is pressurized, the water supply system is prone to leaks. This is especially true of galvanized iron pipe, which has limited resistance to corrosion.

Drain-Waste-Vent System

Drain pipes use gravity to carry waste water away from fixtures, appliances, and other drains. This waste water is carried out of the house to a municipal sewer system or septic tank.

Drain pipes are usually plastic or cast iron. In some older homes, drain pipes may be made of copper or lead. Because they are not part of the supply system, lead drain pipes pose no health hazard. However, lead pipes are no longer manufactured for home plumbing systems.

Drain pipes have diameters ranging from 1¼" to 4". These large diameters allow waste water to pass through easily.

Traps are an important part of the drain system. These curved sections of drain pipe hold standing water, and they are usually found near any drain opening. The standing water of a trap prevents sewer gases from backing up into the home. Each time a drain is used, the standing trap water is flushed away and is replaced by new water.

In order to work properly, the drain system requires air. Air allows waste water to flow freely down drain pipes.

To allow air into the drain system, drain pipes are connected to vent pipes. All drain systems must include vents, and the entire system is called the drain-waste-vent (DWV) system. One or more vent stacks, located on the roof, provide the air needed for the DWV system to work.

Vent

Vent lines

Trap

Drain lines

Out to municipal sewer or septic tank

Planning Your Project

Mapping Your Plumbing System

Mapping your home's plumbing system is a good way to familiarize yourself with the plumbing layout and can help you when planning plumbing renovation projects. With a good map, you can envision the best spots for new fixtures and plan new pipe routes more efficiently. Maps also help in emergencies, when you need to locate burst or leaking pipes quickly.

Draw a plumbing map for each floor on tracing paper, so you can overlay floors and still read the information below. Make your drawings to scale and have all plumbing fixtures marked. Fixture templates and tracing paper are available at drafting supply stores.

Find supply lines inside walls or beneath floors by listening for running water with a stethoscope or a drinking glass while a helper runs water from the fixture. Use fixture locations on the floors above and below to find the general location of pipes.

Tips for Mapping Your Plumbing System

Sweep 90° elbow

90° vent elbow

Waste T

Vent T

Identify drains and vents by the shape of their fittings. Drain pipes (left) feature gradual changes in direction, requiring the use of Y-fittings, waste T-fittings, and sweep 90° elbows. Vents (right) can use fittings with abrupt changes in direction, such as vent T-fittings and vent elbows.

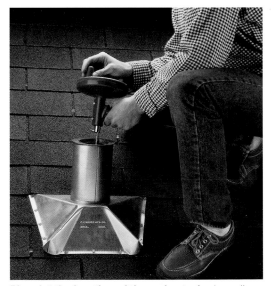

Pinpoint the location of the main stack when all interior walls are finished by jiggling a hand auger down the roof vent while a helper listens to walls from inside the house. Always exercise caution when working on a roof.

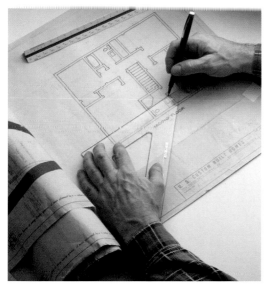

Use floor plans of your house to create your plumbing map. Convert the general outlines for each story to tracing paper. The walls can be drawn larger than scale to fit all the plumbing symbols you will map, but keep overall room dimensions and plumbing fixtures to scale. Be sure to make diagrams for basements and attic spaces as well.

Locate and map all valves throughout the supply lines. This will allow you to shut off only the necessary branches when making repairs, while maintaining service to the rest of the house. Use the correct symbols (right) to identify different valve types (page 40).

Cold water supply	Union
Hot water supply	Coupling
Waste line	
Vent line	Reducer
Waste T	Vent T	Y- fitting
Elbow, 90°	Elbow, 45°	Elbow, sweep 90°
Elbow, facing up	Elbow, facing down
T, outlet facing up	T, outlet facing down
Cap	Plug
Floor drain	Floor cleanout
Ball valve	Gate valve	Check valve
Hose bib	Water heater	Shower
Toilet	Sink	Bathtub

Use standard plumbing symbols on your map to identify the components of your plumbing system. These symbols will help you and your building inspector follow connections and transitions more easily.

How to Map Water Supply Pipes

1 Locate the water meter, usually found along a basement wall. The meter is the first main fitting in the supply line. Mark its location on your basement diagram.

2 Follow the cold water distribution pipe past the main shutoff valve to the water heater, generally the first appliance to receive water. Map the valve and water heater locations on the basement diagram.

3 Locate cold water branch pipes leading to sillcocks, which supply water to hose bibs outside the house. Indicate these branches on the basement map.

4 Return to the water heater and map the location of hot and cold supply lines running to the basement utility fixtures, such as a washing machine and utility sink.

5 Map the routes to any remaining basement plumbing fixtures on your basement diagram. Pipe runs that serve both basement and first-floor plumbing should be marked on both the basement and first-story maps.

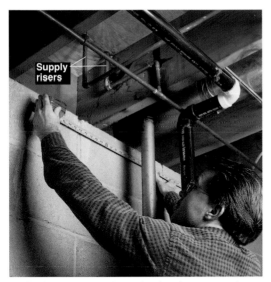

6 Find where vertical supply pipe risers extend up into the floors above. Supply lines generally rise straight to the first-floor fixtures. If there is doubt, measure from the nearest outside wall to the supply line riser, and do the same at the respective first-floor fixture. If measurements are not the same, there is a hidden offset in the pipe route.

7 Map the supply routes to all first-story fixtures by laying the first-floor diagram over the basement map and transferring the locations of vertical supply risers. Indicate any jogs in the supply lines occurring between floors.

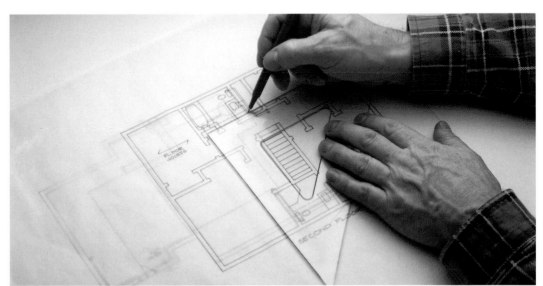

8 Overlay the second-story diagram over the first-floor map, and mark the location of supply pipes—generally they will extend directly up from fixtures below. If first-story and second-story fixtures are not closely aligned, the supply pipes follow an offset route in wall or floor cavities. By overlaying the maps, you can see the relation and distance between fixtures and accurately estimate pipe routes. If no obvious path exists for supply pipes, try locating the pipes by listening in likely areas with a stethoscope (page 18).

How to Map DWV Pipes

1 From the basement, locate the main waste-vent stack and any fixtures that drain directly into it, such as a basement toilet.

2 Determine the path of the main drain under the basement slab by following the main stack to the cleanout hub on the basement floor. The cleanout is usually located near a basement wall facing the street.

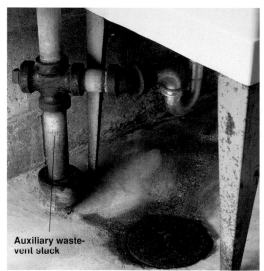

3 Note any auxiliary waste-vent stacks that enter the basement floor. These are typically 2"-diameter pipes, compared to 3"- or 4"-diameter main waste-vent stacks. Auxiliary waste-vent stacks are often located near basement utility sinks or below a kitchen located far from the main stack.

4 On your basement diagram, map the location of the main waste-vent stack, the cleanout hub, and the horizontal main drain pipe. Also note the location of auxiliary stacks, and estimate the path of the horizontal drain pipe connecting the auxiliary stacks to the main drain.

5 From the basement, note the location of horizontal drain pipes running overhead and the points where vertical drain pipes extend up into the floors above. Overlay your first-story diagram onto the basement map, then transfer the location of the vertical waste-vent stacks. Mark the location of all horizontal drain pipes running below the floor.

6 Overlay the second-story diagram over the basement map, transfer the location of the vertical waste-vent stacks, and mark the location of any horizontal drain pipes running beneath the floor. Since the floor spaces between the first and second story are usually finished, you may need to estimate their location. These horizontal drain pipes will usually drain into the nearest waste-vent stack.

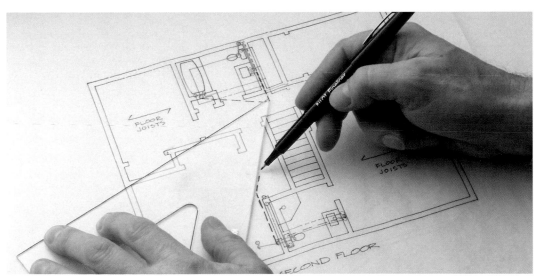

7 Finally, map the location of vent pipes as accurately as you can. If possible, look in your attic to determine where vent pipes emerge from the story below. Indicate whether the individual vent pipes connect to a waste-vent stack or extend through the roofline.

Understanding Plumbing Codes

The plumbing code is the set of regulations that building officials and inspectors use to evaluate your project plans and the quality of your work. Codes vary from region to region, but most are based on the *National Uniform Plumbing Code*, the authority we used in the development of this book.

Code books are available for reference at bookstores and government offices. However, they are highly technical, difficult-to-read manuals. More user-friendly for do-it-yourselfers are the variety of code handbooks available at bookstores and libraries. These handbooks are based on the *National Uniform Plumbing Code* but are easier to read and include many helpful diagrams and photos.

Plumbing code handbooks sometimes discuss three different plumbing "zones" in an effort to accommodate variations in regulations from state to state. The states included in each zone are listed below.

Zone 1: Washington, Oregon, California, Nevada, Idaho, Montana, Wyoming, North Dakota, South Dakota, Minnesota, Iowa, Nebraska, Kansas, Utah, Arizona, Colorado, New Mexico, Indiana, parts of Texas.

Zone 2: Alabama, Arkansas, Louisiana, Tennessee, North Carolina, Mississippi, Georgia, Florida, South Carolina, parts of Texas, parts of Maryland, parts of Delaware, parts of Oklahoma, parts of West Virginia.

Zone 3: Virginia, Kentucky, Missouri, Illinois, Michigan, Ohio, Pennsylvania, New York, Connecticut, Massachusetts, Vermont, New Hampshire, Rhode Island, New Jersey, parts of Delaware, parts of West Virginia, parts of Maine, parts of Maryland, parts of Oklahoma.

Remember that your local plumbing code always supersedes the national code. On some issues, the local code may be less demanding than the national code, but on other issues it may be more restrictive. Your local building inspector is a valuable source of information and may provide you with a convenient summary sheet of the regulations that apply to your project.

The plumbing inspector is the final authority when it comes to evaluating your work. By visually examining and testing your new plumbing, the inspector ensures that your work is safe and functional.

Getting a Permit

To ensure public safety, your community requires that you obtain a permit for most plumbing projects, including most of the projects demonstrated in this book.

When you visit your city building inspection office to apply for a permit, the building official will want to review three drawings of your plumbing project: a site plan, a water supply diagram, and a drain-waste-vent diagram. These drawings are described on this page. If the official is satisfied that your project meets code requirements, he or she will issue you a plumbing permit, which is your legal permission to begin work. The building official also will specify an inspection schedule for your project. As your project nears completion, you will be asked to arrange for an inspector to visit your home while the pipes are exposed to review the installation and ensure its safety.

Although do-it-yourselfers often complete complex plumbing projects without obtaining a permit or having the work inspected, we strongly urge you to comply with the legal requirements in your area. A flawed plumbing system can be dangerous, and it can potentially threaten the value of your home.

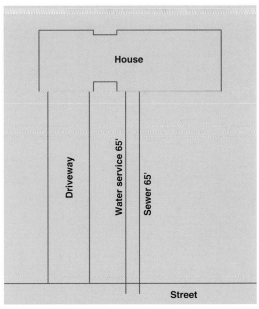

The site plan shows the location of the water main and sewer main with respect to your yard and home. The distances from your foundation to the water main and from the foundation to the main sewer should be indicated on the site plan.

The supply riser diagram shows the length of the hot and cold water pipes and the relation of the fixtures to one another. The inspector will use this diagram to determine the proper size for the new water supply pipes in your system.

A DWV diagram shows the routing of drain and vent pipes in your system. Make sure to indicate the lengths of drain pipes and the distances between fixtures. The inspector will use this diagram to determine if you have properly sized the drain traps, drain pipes, and vent pipes in your project.

Sizing for Water Distribution Pipes

Fixture	Unit rating	Size of service pipe from street	Size of distribution pipe from water meter	Maximum length (ft.)—total fixture units					
				40	60	80	100	150	200
Toilet	3								
Vanity sink	1								
Shower	2	¾"	½"	9	8	7	6	5	4
Bathtub	2								
Dishwasher	2	¾"	¾"	27	23	19	17	14	11
Kitchen sink	2	¾"	1"	44	40	36	33	28	23
Clothes washer	2								
Utility sink	2	1"	1"	60	47	41	36	30	25
Sillcock	3	1"	1¼"	102	87	76	67	52	44

Water distribution pipes are the main pipes extending from the water meter throughout the house, supplying water to the branch pipes leading to individual fixtures. To determine the size of the distribution pipes, you must first calculate the total demand in "fixture units" (above, left) and the overall length of the water supply lines, from the street hookup through the water meter and to the most distant fixture in the house. Then, use the second table (above, right) to calculate the minimum size for the water distribution pipes. Note that the fixture unit capacity depends partly on the size of the street-side pipe that delivers water to your meter.

Sizes for Branch Pipes & Supply Tubes

Fixture	Min. branch pipe size	Min. supply tube size
Toilet	½"	⅜"
Vanity sink	½"	⅜"
Shower	½"	½"
Bathtub	½"	½"
Dishwasher	½"	½"
Kitchen sink	½"	½"
Clothes washer	½"	½"
Utility sink	½"	½"
Sillcock	¾"	N.A.
Water heater	¾"	N.A.

Branch pipes are the water supply lines that run from the distribution pipes toward the individual fixtures. **Supply tubes** are the vinyl, chromed copper, or braided tubes that carry water from the branch pipes to the fixtures. Use the chart above as a guide when sizing branch pipes and supply tubes.

Valve Requirements

Main shutoff

Water meter

Full-bore ball valve on house side

Full-bore gate valves or ball valves are required in the following locations: on both the street side and house side of the water meter; on the inlet pipes for water heaters and heating system boilers. Individual fixtures should have accessible shutoff valves, but these need not be full-bore valves. All sillcocks must have individual control valves located inside the house.

Modifying Water Pressure

Pressure-reducing valve

Pressure-reducing valve (shown above) is required if the water pressure coming into your home is greater than 80 pounds per square inch (psi). The reducing valve should be installed near the point where the water service enters the building. A **booster pump** may be required if the water pressure in your home is below 40 psi.

Preventing Water Hammer

Water hammer arresters may be required by code. Water hammer is a problem that may occur when the fast-acting valves on washing machines or other appliances trap air and cause pipes to vibrate against framing members. The arrester works as a shock absorber and has a watertight diaphragm inside. It is mounted to a T-fitting installed near the appliance (see page 294).

Anti-siphon Devices

Vacuum breaker

Vacuum breakers must be installed on all indoor and outdoor hose bibs and any outdoor branch pipes that run underground (page 177, step 7). Vacuum breakers prevent contaminated water from being drawn into the water supply pipes in the event of a sudden drop in water pressure in the water main. When a drop in pressure produces a partial vacuum, the breaker prevents siphoning by allowing air to enter the pipes.

Pipe Support Intervals

Type of pipe	Vertical-run support interval	Horizontal-run support interval
Copper	10 ft.	6 ft.
PEX	5 ft.	3 ft.
CPVC	10 ft.	3 ft.
PVC	10 ft.	4 ft.
Steel	12 ft.	10 ft.
Iron	15 ft.	5 ft.

Drain cleanouts make your DWV system easier to service. In most areas, the plumbing code requires that you place cleanouts at the end of every horizontal drain run. Where horizontal runs are not accessible, removable drain traps will suffice as cleanouts.

Minimum intervals for supporting pipes are determined by the type of pipe and its orientation in the system. See page 40 for acceptable pipe support materials. Remember that the measurements shown above are minimum requirements; local code may require supports at closer intervals.

Fixture Units & Minimum Trap Size

Fixture	Fixture units	Min. trap size
Shower	2	2"
Vanity sink	1	1¼"
Bathtub	2	1½"
Dishwasher	2	1½"
Kitchen sink	2	1½"
Kitchen sink*	3	1½"
Clothes washer	2	1½"
Utility sink	2	1½"
Floor drain	1	2"

*Kitchen sink with attached food disposer

Minimum trap size for fixtures is determined by the drain fixture unit rating, a unit of measure assigned by the plumbing code. NOTE: Kitchen sinks rate 3 units if they include an attached food disposer, 2 units otherwise.

Sizes for Horizontal & Vertical Drain Pipes

Pipe size	Maximum fixture units for horizontal branch drain	Maximum fixture units for vertical drain stacks
1¼"	1	2
1½"	3	4
2"	6	10
2½"	12	20
3"	20	30
4"	160	240

Drain pipe sizes are determined by the load on the pipes, as measured by the total fixture units. Horizontal drain pipes less than 3" in diameter should slope ¼" per foot toward the main drain. Pipes 3" or more in diameter should slope ⅛" per foot. NOTE: Horizontal or vertical drain pipes for a toilet must be 3" or larger.

Vent Pipe Sizes, Critical Distances

Size of fixture drain	Minimum vent pipe size	Maximum critical distance
1¼"	1¼"	2½ ft.
1½"	1¼"	3½ ft.
2"	1½"	5 ft.
3"	2"	6 ft.
4"	3"	10 ft.

Vent pipes are usually one pipe size smaller than the drain pipes they serve. Code requires that the distance between the drain trap and the vent pipe fall within a maximum "critical distance," a measurement that is determined by the size of the fixture drain. Use this chart to determine both the minimum size for the vent pipe and the maximum critical distance.

Vent Pipe Orientation to Drain Pipe

Vent pipes must extend in an upward direction from drains, no less than 45° from horizontal. This ensures that waste water cannot flow into the vent pipe and block it. At the opposite end, a new vent pipe should connect to an existing vent pipe or main waste-vent stack at a point at least 6" above the highest fixture draining into the system.

Wet Venting

Wet vents are pipes that serve as a vent for one fixture and a drain for another. The sizing of a wet vent is based on the total fixture units it supports (opposite page): a 3" wet vent can serve up to 12 fixture units; a 2" wet vent is rated for 4 fixture units; a 1½" wet vent, for only 1 fixture unit. NOTE: The distance between the wet-vented fixture and the wet vent itself must be no more than the maximum critical distance (chart above).

Auxiliary Venting

Fixtures must have an auxiliary vent if the distance to the main waste-vent stack exceeds the critical distance (chart above). A toilet, for example, should have a separate vent pipe if it is located more than 6 ft. from the main waste-vent stack. This secondary vent pipe should connect to the stack or an existing vent pipe at a point at least 6" above the highest fixture on the system.

A pressure gauge and air pump are used to test DWV lines. The system is first blocked off at each fixture and at points near where the new drain and vent pipes connect to the main stack. Air is then pumped into the system to a pressure of 5 pounds per square inch (psi). To pass inspection, the system must hold this pressure for 15 minutes.

Testing New Plumbing Pipes

When the building inspector comes to review your new plumbing, he or she may require that you perform a pressure test on the DWV and water supply lines as he or she watches. The inspection and test should be performed after the system is completed but before the new pipes are covered with wallboard. To ensure that the inspection goes smoothly, it is a good idea to perform your own pretest, so you can locate and repair any problems before the inspector visits.

The DWV system is tested by blocking off the new drain and vent pipes, then pressuring the system with air to see if it leaks. At the fixture stub-outs, the DWV pipes can be capped off or plugged with test balloons designed for this purpose. The air pump, pressure gauge, and test balloons required to test the DWV system can be obtained at tool rental centers.

Testing the water supply lines is a simple matter of turning on the water and examining the joints for leaks. If you find a leak, you will have to drain the pipes, then remake the faulty joints.

How to Test New DWV Pipes

1 Insert a test balloon into the test T-fittings at the top and bottom of the new DWV line, blocking the pipes entirely. NOTE: Ordinary T-fittings installed near the bottom of the drain line and near the top of the vent line are generally used for test fittings.

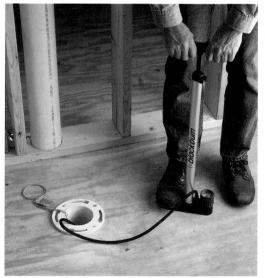

2 Block toilet drains with a test balloon designed for a closet bend. Large test balloons may have to be inflated with an air pump.

3 Cap off the remaining fixture drains by solvent-gluing test caps onto the stub-outs. After the system is tested, these caps are simply knocked loose with a hammer.

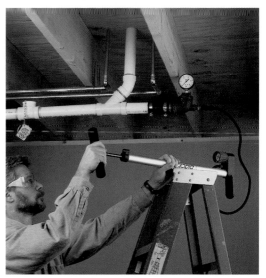

4 At a cleanout fitting, insert a *weenie*—a special test balloon with an air gauge and inflation valve. Attach an air pump to the valve on the weenie and pressurize the pipes to 5 psi. Watch the pressure gauge for 15 minutes to ensure that the system does not lose pressure.

5 If the DWV system loses air when pressurized, check each joint for leaks by rubbing soapy water over the fittings and looking for active bubbles. When you identify a problem joint, cut away the existing fitting and solvent-glue a new fitting in place, using couplings and short lengths of pipe.

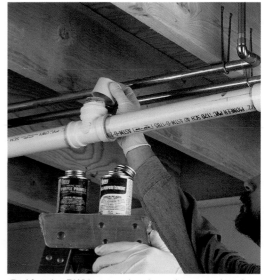

6 After the DWV system has been inspected and approved by a building official, remove the test balloons and close the test T-fittings by solvent-gluing caps onto the open inlets.

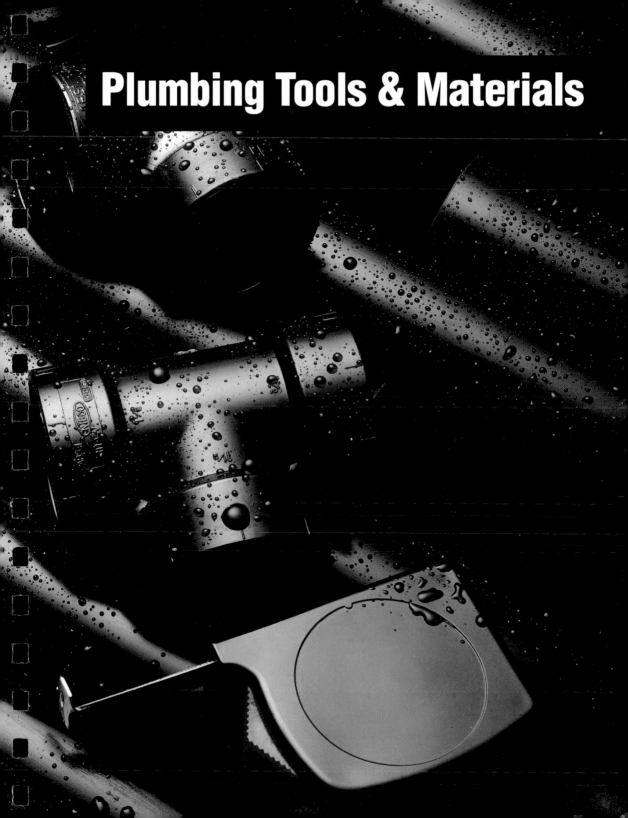

Plumbing Tools & Materials

Tools for Plumbing

Many plumbing projects and repairs can be completed with basic hand tools you probably already own. Adding a few simple plumbing tools will prepare you for all the projects in this book. Specialty tools, such as a snap cutter or appliance dolly, are available at rental centers. When buying tools, invest in quality products.

Always care for tools properly. Clean tools after using them, wiping them free of dirt and dust with a soft rag. Prevent rust on metal tools by wiping them with a rag dipped in household oil. If a metal tool gets wet, dry it immediately, and then wipe it with an oiled rag. Keep toolboxes and cabinets organized. Make sure all tools are stored securely.

Caulk gun is designed to hold tubes of caulk or glue. A squeeze handle pushes a steady bead of caulk or glue out of the nozzle.

Flashlight is an indispensable plumber's helper for inspecting pipes and drain openings.

Circuit tester is an important safety device that allows the user to test for live current in an electrical outlet or appliance. Also referred to as testing for hot wires.

Ratchet wrench is used for tightening or loosening bolts and nuts. It has interchangeable sockets for adapting to different-sized bolts or nuts.

Hacksaw is used for cutting metals. Also can be used for cutting plastic pipes. Has replaceable blades.

Small wire brush has soft brass bristles for cleaning metals without damaging surfaces.

Cold chisel is used with a *ball peen hammer* to cut or chip ceramic tile, mortar, or hardened metals.

Utility knife has a razor-sharp blade for cutting a wide variety of materials. Useful for trimming ends of plastic pipes. For safety, the utility knife should have a retractable blade.

Files are used to smooth the edges of metal, wood, or plastic. The *round file* (top) can be used to remove burrs from the insides of pipes. The *flat file* is used for all general smoothing tasks.

Ball peen hammer is made for striking metallic objects, like a *cold chisel*. The head of a ball peen hammer is made to resist chipping.

Screwdrivers include the two most common types: the *slotted* (top), and the *Phillips*.

Adjustable wrench has a movable jaw that permits the wrench to fit a wide variety of bolt heads or nuts.

Channel-type pliers has a movable handle that allows the jaws to be adjusted for maximum gripping strength. The insides of the jaws are serrated to prevent slipping.

Wooden mallet is used for striking nonmetallic objects, such as plastic drywall anchors.

Needlenose pliers has thin jaws for gripping small objects or for reaching into confined areas.

Putty knife is especially helpful for scraping away old putty or caulk from appliances and fixtures.

Tape measure should have a retractable steel blade at least 16 feet long.

Level is used for setting new appliances and checking the slope of exhaust ducts.

Tubing cutter makes straight, smooth cuts in plastic and copper pipe. A tubing cutter usually has a dull, triangular blade, called a *reaming tip*, for removing burrs from the insides of pipes.

Closet auger is used to clear toilet clogs. It is a slender tube with a crank handle on one end of a flexible auger cable. A special bend in the tube allows the auger to be positioned in the bottom of the toilet bowl. The bend is usually protected with a rubber sleeve to prevent scratching the toilet.

Plastic tubing cutter works like a gardener's pruners to cut flexible plastic pipes quickly.

Spud wrench is specially designed for removing or tightening large nuts that are 2" to 4" in diameter. Hooks on the ends of the wrench grab onto the *lugs* of large nuts for increased leverage.

Plunger clears drain clogs with water and air pressure. The *flanged plunger* (shown) is used for toilet bowls. The flange usually can be folded up into the cup for use as a *standard plunger*. Use a standard plunger to clear clogs in sinks, tubs, showers, and floor drains.

Hand auger, sometimes called a *snake*, is used to clear clogs in drain lines. A long, flexible steel cable is stored in the disk-shaped crank. A pistol-grip handle allows the user to apply steady pressure on the cable.

Blow bag, sometimes called an *expansion nozzle*, is used to clear drains. It attaches to a garden hose and removes clogs with powerful spurts of water. The blow bag is best used on floor drains.

Propane torch (left) is used for soldering fittings to copper pipes. Light the torch quickly and safely using a **spark lighter** (above).

³⁄₈" power drill

Power screwdriver

Reciprocating saw

Power hand tools can make any job faster, easier, and safer. Cordless power tools offer added convenience. Use a cordless ³⁄₈" **power drill** for virtually any drilling task.

Motorized drain auger

Power miter box

Right-angle drill

Appliance dolly

Snap cutter

Pipe wrench has a movable jaw that adjusts to fit a variety of pipe diameters. Pipe wrench is used for tightening and loosening pipes, pipe fittings, and large nuts. Two pipe wrenches often are used together to prevent damage to pipes and fittings.

Rental tools may be needed for large jobs and special situations. A **power miter box** makes fast, accurate cuts in a wide variety of materials, including plastic pipes. A **motorized drain auger** clears tree roots from sewer service lines. Use an **appliance dolly** to move heavy objects like water heaters. A **snap cutter** is designed to cut tough cast-iron pipes. The **right-angle drill** is useful for drilling holes in hard-to-reach areas.

Plumbing Materials

Check local plumbing code for materials allowed in your area. All diameters specified are the interior diameters (I.D.) of pipes.

Benefits & Characteristics

Cast iron is very strong but is difficult to cut and fit. Repairs and replacements should be made with plastic pipe, if allowed by local code.

ABS (acrylonitrile butadiene styrene) was once approved for use in DWV systems. Most local codes now prohibit ABS for new installations, but in some cases it can be added to pre-existing ABS DWV systems.

PVC (polyvinyl chloride) is a modern rigid plastic that is highly resistant to damage by heat or chemicals. It is the best material for drain-waste-vent pipes.

Brass is heavy and durable. **Chromed brass** has an attractive shiny surface and is used for drain traps where appearance is important.

CPVC (chlorinated polyvinyl chloride) rigid plastic is engineered to withstand the high temperatures and pressures of supply systems. Pipes and fittings are inexpensive.

Galvanized iron is very strong but gradually will corrode. Not advised for new installation. Because galvanized iron is difficult to cut and fit, large jobs are best left to a professional.

Rigid copper is the best material for water supply pipes. It resists corrosion and has smooth surfaces that provide good water flow. Soldered copper joints are very durable.

Chromed copper has an attractive shiny surface and is used in areas where appearance is important. Chromed copper is durable and easy to bend and fit.

PE (polyethylene) plastic is a black or bluish flexible pipe sometimes used for main water service lines as well as irrigation systems.

Flexible copper tubing is easy to shape and will withstand a slight frost without rupturing. Flexible copper bends easily, so it requires fewer fittings than rigid copper.

PEX (cross-linked polyethylene) is flexible enough to make curves and turns simply by bending, but it is also strong enough that it is approved by all major building codes as a general water supply pipe—hot or cold.

Common Uses	Lengths	Diameters	Fitting Methods	Tools Used for Cutting
Main drain-waste-vent pipes	5 ft., 10 ft.	3", 4"	banded neoprene couplings	Snap cutter or hacksaw
Pipes; drain traps	Sold by linear ft.	2", 3", 4"	Glue and plastic	Miter box or hacksaw
Drain & vent pipes; drain traps	10 ft., 20 ft.; or sold by linear ft.	1¼", 1½", 2", 3", 4"	Solvent glue and plastic fittings	Tubing cutter, miter box, or hacksaw
Valves & shutoffs; chromed drain traps	Lengths vary	¼", ½", ¾", For drain traps: 1¼", 1½"	Compression fittings, or with metal solder	Tubing cutter, hacksaw, or reciprocating saw
Hot & cold water supply pipes	10 ft.	⅜", ½", ¾", 1"	Solvent glue and plastic fittings, or with grip fittings	Tubing cutter, miter box, or hacksaw
Drains; hot & cold water supply pipes	1" to 1-ft. nipples; custom lengths up to 20 ft.	½", ¾", 1", 1½", 2"	Galvanized threaded fittings	Hacksaw or reciprocating saw
Hot & cold water supply pipes	10 ft., 20 ft.; or sold by linear ft.	⅜", ½", ¾", 1"	Metal solder or compression fittings	Tubing cutter, hacksaw, or jig saw
Supply tubing for plumbing fixtures	12", 20", 30"	⅜"	Brass compression fittings	Tubing cutter or hacksaw
Outdoor cold water supply pipes	Sold in coils of 25 to hundreds of ft.	¼" to 1"	Rigid PVC fittings and stainless steel hose clamps	Ratchet-style plastic pipe cutter or miter saw
Gas tubing; hot & cold water supply tubing	30-ft., 60-ft. coils; or sold by linear ft.	¼", ⅜", ½", ¾", 1"	Brass flare fittings, compression fittings, or metal solder	Tubing cutter or hacksaw
Hot and cold supply pipes in homes and recreational vehicles; tubing for radiant floor systems.	Sold in coils of 25 to hundreds of ft.	¼" to 1"	Crimp fittings	Tubing cutter

Water supply fittings are available in copper (top), CPVC plastic (center), and PEX (bottom). Fittings for CPVC and copper are available in many shapes, including: unions (A), reducers (B), 90° elbows (C), reducing elbows (D), 45° elbows (E), T-fittings (F), reducing T-fittings (G), drop-ear elbows (H), threaded adapters (I), and caps (J). Common PEX fittings (bottom) include unions (K), PEX-to-copper unions (L), 90° elbows (M), T-fittings (N), plugs (O), drop-ear elbows (P), and threaded adapters (M).

Water supply valves are available in brass or plastic and in a variety of styles, including: drain-and-waste valves (A), gate valve (B), full-bore ball valves (C), fixture shutoff valve (D), vacuum breaker (E), and hose bib (F).

Support materials for pipes include: plastic pipe hangers (A), copper J-hooks (B), copper wire hangers (C), riser clamp (D), plastic pipe straps (E), copper pipe straps (F), flexible copper, steel, and plastic pipe strapping (G, H, I). Do not mix metal types when supporting metal pipes; use copper support materials for copper pipe, and steel for steel and cast-iron pipes.

Vent elbow

Vent T (must connect to waste-vent stack at a point at least 6" above the highest fixture)

Vent pipes

Waste T-fitting

P-trap

Drain pipes

Low-heel vent 90°

Closet bend

Cleanout

Y-fitting with 45° elbow (combo)

Y-fitting with 45° elbow

Main waste stack

Cleanout

Y-fitting

Basic DWV tree shows the correct orientation of drain and vent fittings in a plumbing system. Bends in the vent pipes can be very sharp, but drain pipes should use fittings with a noticeable sweep. Fittings used to direct falling waste water from a vertical to a horizontal pipe should have bends that are even more sweeping. Your local plumbing code may require that you install cleanout fittings where vertical drain pipes meet horizontal runs.

DWV Fittings

Use the photos on these pages to identify the DWV fittings specified in the project how-to directions found later in this book. Each fitting shown is available in a variety of sizes to match your needs. Always use fittings made from the same material as your DWV pipes.

DWV fittings come in a variety of shapes to serve different functions within the plumbing system.

Vents: In general, the fittings used to connect vent pipes have very sharp bends with no sweep. Vent fittings include the vent T and vent 90° elbow. Standard drain pipe fittings can also be used to join vent pipes.

Horizontal-to-vertical drains: To change directions in a drain pipe from the horizontal to the vertical, use fittings with a noticeable sweep. Standard fittings for this use include waste T-fittings and 90° elbows. Y-fittings and 45° and 22½° elbows can also be used for this purpose.

Vertical-to-horizontal drains: To change directions from the vertical to the horizontal, use fittings with a very pronounced, gradual sweep. Common fittings for this purpose include the long-radius T-Y-fitting and some Y-fittings with 45° elbows.

Horizontal offsets in drains: Y-fittings, 45° elbows, 22½° elbows, and long sweep 90° elbows are used when changing directions in horizontal pipe runs. Whenever possible, horizontal drain pipes should use gradual, sweeping bends rather than sharp turns.

T-fittings

Low-heel vent 90°

Waste T

Vent T

Waste T with additional side inlet

Waste cross

Elbows

Long sweep 90° elbow

90° elbow

Vent elbow

Closet bend

Street elbow

Reducing elbow

22½° elbow

45° elbow

Y-fittings

Y with 45° elbow (combo)

Y with cleanout plug

Reducing Y-fitting

Y-fitting

Specialty Fittings

Test caps

Cap

Cleanout plug

P-trap with slip fittings

Banded clamp

P-trap with solvent-glued fittings

Coupling

Reducer

Reducing bushing

Fittings for DWV pipes are available in many configurations, with openings ranging from 1¼" to 4" in diameter. When planning your project, buy plentiful numbers of DWV and water supply fittings from a reputable retailer with a good return policy. It is much more efficient to return leftover materials after you complete your project than it is to interrupt your work each time you need to shop for a missing fitting.

Connect plastic to cast iron with banded couplings (pages 74 to 77). Rubber sleeves cover ends of pipes and ensure a watertight joint.

Connect plastic to threaded metal pipes with male and female threaded adapters. Plastic adapter is solvent-glued to plastic pipe. Threads of pipe should be wrapped with Teflon tape. Metal pipe is then screwed directly to the adapter.

Connect copper to galvanized iron with a dielectric union. A dielectric union is threaded onto iron pipe and is soldered to copper pipe. A dielectric union has a plastic spacer that prevents corrosion caused by an electro-chemical reaction between dissimilar metals.

Connect metal hot water pipe to plastic with a hot water transition fitting that prevents leaks caused by different expansion rates of materials. Metal pipe threads are wrapped with Teflon tape. Plastic pipe is solvent-glued to fitting.

Connect a water pipe to any fixture supply tube, using a shutoff valve (pages 224 to 225).

Connect any supply tube to a fixture tailpiece with a coupling nut. Coupling nut seals the bell-shaped end of supply tube against the fixture tailpiece.

Connect a supply tube to copper pipe with a saddle valve (page 239). A saddle valve (shown cutaway) often is used to connect a refrigerator icemaker. Some codes prohibit the use of saddle valves.

Working with Copper

Copper is the ideal material for water supply pipes. It resists corrosion and has smooth surfaces that provide good water flow. Copper pipes are available in several diameters (page 39), but most home water supply systems use ½" or ¾" pipe. Copper pipe is manufactured in rigid and flexible forms.

Rigid copper, sometimes called hard copper, is approved for home water supply systems by all local codes. It comes in three wall-thickness grades: Types M, L, and K. Type M is the thinnest, the least expensive, and a good choice for do-it-yourself home plumbing.

Rigid Type L usually is required by code for commercial plumbing systems. Because it is strong and solders easily, Type L may be preferred by some professional plumbers and do-it-yourselfers for home use. Type K has the heaviest wall thickness and is used most often for underground water service lines.

Flexible copper, also called soft copper, comes in two wall-thickness grades: Types L and K. Both are approved for most home water supply systems, although flexible Type L copper is used primarily for gas service lines. Because it is bendable and will resist a mild frost, Type L may be installed as part of a water supply system in unheated indoor areas, like crawl spaces. Type K is used for underground water service lines.

A third form of copper, called DWV, is used for drain systems. Because most codes now allow low-cost plastic pipes for drain systems, DWV copper is seldom used.

Copper pipes are connected with soldered, compression, or flare fittings (see chart below). Always follow your local code for the correct types of pipes and fittings allowed in your area.

Soldered fittings, also called sweat fittings, often are used to join copper pipes. Correctly soldered fittings (pages 46 to 50) are strong and trouble-free. Copper pipe can also be joined with compression fittings (pages 52 to 53) or flare fittings (pages 54 to 55). See chart below.

Copper Pipe & Fitting Chart

Fitting Method	Rigid Copper			Flexible Copper		General Comments
	Type M	Type L	Type K	Type L	Type K	
Soldered	yes	yes	yes	yes	yes	Inexpensive, strong, and trouble-free fitting method. Requires some skill.
Compression	yes	not recommended		yes	yes	Easy to use. Allows pipes or fixtures to be repaired or replaced readily. More expensive than solder. Best used on flexible copper.
Flare	no	no	no	yes	yes	Use only with flexible copper pipes. Usually used as a gas-line fitting. Requires some skill.

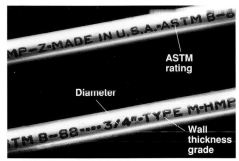

Grade stamp information includes the pipe diameter, the wall-thickness grade, and a stamp of approval from the ASTM (American Society for Testing and Materials). Type M pipe is identified by red lettering, Type L by blue lettering.

Specialty tools & materials for working with copper include: flaring tools (A), emery cloth (B), coil-spring tubing bender (C), pipe joint compound (D), self-cleaning soldering paste (flux) (E), lead-free solder (F), wire brush (G), flux brush (H), compression fitting (I), flare fitting (J).

Bend flexible copper pipe with a coil-spring tubing bender to avoid kinks. Select a bender that matches the outside diameter of the pipe. Slip bender over pipe using a twisting motion. Bend pipe slowly until it reaches the correct angle, but not more than 90°.

Find length of copper pipe needed by measuring between the bottom of the copper fitting sockets (fittings shown in cutaway). Mark length on the pipe with a felt-tipped pen.

Cutting & Soldering Copper

The best way to cut rigid and flexible copper pipe is with a tubing cutter. A tubing cutter makes a smooth, straight cut, an important first step toward making a watertight joint. Remove any metal burrs on the cut edges with a reaming tool or round file.

Copper can be cut with a hacksaw. A hacksaw is useful in tight areas where a tubing cutter will not fit. Take care to make a smooth, straight cut when cutting with a hacksaw.

A soldered pipe joint, also called a sweated joint, is made by heating a copper or brass fitting with a propane torch until the fitting is just hot enough to melt metal solder. The heat draws the solder into the gap between the fitting and pipe to form a watertight seal. A fitting that is overheated or unevenly heated will not draw in solder. Copper pipes and fittings must be clean and dry to form a watertight seal.

Everything You Need

Tools: tubing cutter with reaming tip (or hacksaw and round file), wire brush, flux brush, propane torch, spark lighter (or matches), adjustable wrench, channel-type pliers.

Materials: copper pipe, copper fittings, emery cloth, soldering paste (flux), sheet metal, lead-free solder, rag.

Protect wood from heat of the torch flame while soldering, using a double layer (two 18" × 18" pieces) of 26-gauge sheet metal. Buy sheet metal at hardware stores or building supply centers and keep it to use with all soldering projects.

Soldering Tips

Use caution when soldering copper. Pipes and fittings become very hot and must be allowed to cool before handling.

Keep joint dry when soldering existing water pipes by plugging the pipe with bread. Bread absorbs moisture that may ruin the soldering process and cause pinhole leaks. The bread dissolves when water is turned back on.

Torch valve

Prevent accidents by shutting off propane torch immediately after use. Make sure valve is closed completely.

1 Place tubing cutter over the pipe and tighten the handle so that pipe rests on both rollers, and cutting wheel is on marked line.

Cutting wheel

Roller

2 Turn tubing cutter one rotation so that cutting wheel scores a continuous straight line around the pipe.

3 Rotate the cutter in the opposite direction, tightening the handle slightly after every two rotations, until cut is complete.

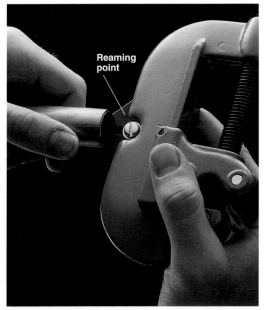

Reaming point

4 Remove sharp metal burrs from inside edge of the cut pipe, using the reaming point on the tubing cutter, or a round file.

How to Solder Copper Pipes & Fittings

1 Clean end of each pipe by sanding with emery cloth. Ends must be free of dirt and grease to ensure that the solder forms a good seal.

2 Clean inside of each fitting by scouring with a wire brush or emery cloth.

3 Apply a thin layer of soldering paste (flux) to end of each pipe, using a flux brush. Soldering paste should cover about 1" of pipe end.

4 Assemble each joint by inserting the pipe into the fitting so it is tight against the bottom of the fitting sockets. Twist each fitting slightly to spread soldering paste.

5 Prepare the wire solder by unwinding 8" to 10" of wire from spool. Bend the first 2" of the wire to a 90° angle.

6 Open the gas valve and trigger the spark lighter to ignite the torch.

7 Adjust the torch valve until the inner portion of the flame is 1" to 2" long.

Fitting

Pipe

Pipe

8 Hold flame tip against middle of fitting for 4 to 5 seconds, until soldering paste begins to sizzle.

9 Heat other side of copper fitting to ensure that heat is distributed evenly. Touch solder to pipe. If solder melts, pipe is ready to be soldered.

(continued next page)

How to Solder Copper Pipes & Fittings (continued)

10 When pipe is hot enough to melt solder, remove torch and quickly push ½" to ¾" of solder into each joint. Capillary action fills joint with liquid solder. A correctly soldered joint should show a thin bead of solder around the lip of the fitting.

11 Allow the joint to cool briefly, then wipe away excess solder with a dry rag. **Caution: Pipes will be hot.** If joints leak after water is turned on, disassemble and resolder.

How to Solder Brass Valves

1 Remove the valve stem with an adjustable wrench. Removing the stem prevents heat damage to rubber or plastic stem parts while soldering. Prepare the copper pipes (page 48) and assemble joints.

2 Light propane torch (page 49). Heat body of valve, moving flame to distribute heat evenly. Brass is denser than copper, so it requires more heating time before joints will draw solder. Apply solder (pages 48 to 50). Let metal cool, then reassemble valve.

How to Take Apart Soldered Joints

1 Turn off the water (page 12) and drain the pipes by opening the highest and lowest faucets in the house. Light propane torch (page 49). Hold flame tip to the fitting until the solder becomes shiny and begins to melt.

2 Use channel-type pliers to separate the pipes from the fitting.

3 Remove old solder by heating ends of pipe with propane torch. Use dry rag to wipe away melted solder quickly. **Caution:** Pipes will be hot.

4 Use emery cloth to polish ends of pipe down to bare metal. Never reuse old fittings.

Compression
nut

Compression
ring

Compression
nut

Compression
ring

Copper
pipe

Compression fitting (shown in cutaway) shows how threaded compression nut forms seal by forcing the compression ring against the copper pipe. Compression ring is covered with pipe joint compound before assembling to ensure a perfect seal.

Using Compression Fittings

Compression fittings are used to make connections that may need to be taken apart. Compression fittings are easy to disconnect and often are used to install supply tubes and fixture shutoff valves (pages 224 to 225, and sequence below). Use compression fittings in places where it is unsafe or difficult to solder, such as in crawl spaces.

Compression fittings are used most often with flexible copper pipe. Flexible copper is soft enough to allow the compression ring to seat snugly, creating a watertight seal. Compression fittings also may be used to make connections with Type M rigid copper pipe. See the chart on page 44.

Everything You Need

Tools: felt-tipped pen, tubing cutter or hacksaw, adjustable wrenches.

Materials: brass compression fittings, pipe joint compound or Teflon tape.

How to Attach Supply Tubes to Fixture Shutoff Valves with Compression Fittings

Flexible
copper
supply
tube

1 Bend flexible copper supply tube and mark to length. Include ½" for portion that will fit inside valve. Cut tube (page 47).

Compression
ring

Compression
nut

2 Slide the compression nut and then the compression ring over end of the pipe. The threads of the nut should face the valve.

3 Apply a layer of pipe joint compound or Teflon tape over the threads on the valve. This helps ensure a watertight seal.

4 Insert the end of the pipe into the fitting so it fits flush against the bottom of the fitting socket.

5 Slide the compression ring and nut against the threads of the valve. Hand-tighten the nut onto the valve.

6 Tighten the compression nut with adjustable wrenches. Do not overtighten. Turn on the water and watch for leaks. If the fitting leaks, tighten the nut gently.

How to Join Two Copper Pipes with a Compression Union Fitting

1 Slide compression nuts and rings over the ends of pipes. Place a threaded union between the pipes.

2 Apply a layer of pipe joint compound or Teflon tape to the union's threads, then screw compression nuts onto the union.

3 Hold the center of the union fitting with an adjustable wrench and use another wrench to tighten each compression nut one complete turn. Turn on the water. If the fitting leaks, tighten the nuts gently.

Flare
nut

Flared end of pipe

Brass
union
fitting

Flare
nut

Flared end of pipe

Flexible copper pipe

Using Flare Fittings

Flare fittings are used more often for flexible copper gas lines. Flare fittings may be used with flexible copper water supply pipes, but they cannot be used where the connections will be concealed inside walls. Always check your local code regarding the use of flare fittings.

Flare fittings are easy to disconnect. Use flare fittings in places where it is unsafe or difficult to solder, such as in crawl spaces.

Everything You Need

Tools: two-piece flaring tool, adjustable wrenches.

Materials: brass flare fittings.

Flare fitting (shown in cutaway) shows how flared end of flexible copper pipe forms seal against the head of a brass union fitting.

How to Join Two Copper Pipes with a Flare Union Fitting

Flare
nuts

1 Slide flare nuts onto ends of pipes. Nuts must be placed on pipes before ends can be flared. Ream inside of pipe to create smooth edge.

Flaring
tool
base

2 Select hole in flaring tool base that matches outside diameter of pipe. Open base, and place end of pipe inside hole.

Flare nut

Flaring tip

Yoke

3 Clamp pipe inside flaring tool base. End of pipe must be flush with flat surface of base.

4 Slip yoke of flaring tool around base. Center flaring tip of yoke over end of pipe (inset photo above). Tighten handle of yoke to shape the end of the pipe. Flare is completed when handle cannot be turned further.

5 Remove yoke and remove pipe from base. Repeat flaring for other pipe.

6 Place flare union between flared ends of pipe and screw flare nuts onto union.

7 Hold center of flare union with adjustable wrench and use another wrench to tighten flare nuts one complete turn. Turn on water. If fitting leaks, tighten nuts.

Working with Plastics

Plastic pipes and fittings are popular with do-it-yourselfers because they are lightweight, inexpensive, and easy to use. Most local plumbing codes now allow the use of plastics for home plumbing.

Plastic pipes are available in rigid and flexible forms. Rigid plastics include ABS (acrylonitrile butadiene styrene), PVC (polyvinyl chloride), and CPVC (chlorinated polyvinyl chloride). The most commonly used flexible plastics are PE (polyethylene) and PEX (cross-linked polyethylene).

ABS and PVC are used in drain systems. ABS is no longer approved for new installations. PVC resists chemical damage and heat better than ABS. It is approved for above-ground use by all plumbing codes. However, some codes still require cast-iron pipe for main drains that run under concrete slabs. CPVC is used in water supply systems.

PE is used in outdoor plumbing. PEX is approved for all indoor supply applications.

Plastic pipes can be joined to existing iron or copper pipes using transition fittings (page 43), but different types of plastics should not be joined. For example, if your drain pipes are PVC plastic, use only PVC pipes and fittings when making repairs and replacements.

Prolonged exposure to sunlight eventually can weaken plastic plumbing pipe, so plastics should not be installed or stored in areas that receive constant direct sunlight.

Metal pipe

Metal pipe

Jumper wire

Ground clamp

Plastic pipe

Caution: Your home electrical system could be grounded through metal water pipes. When adding plastic pipes to a metal plumbing system, make sure the electrical ground circuit is not broken. Use ground clamps and jumper wires, available at any hardware store, to bypass the plastic transition and complete the electrical ground circuit. Clamps must be firmly attached to bare metal on both sides of the plastic pipe.

Solvent-glued fittings are used on rigid plastic pipes. Solvent dissolves a thin layer of plastic and bonds the pipe and fitting together.

Grip fittings are used to join CPVC pipe. Each fitting has a metal grip ring, plastic compression ring, and rubber O-ring.

Plastic Pipe Grade Stamps

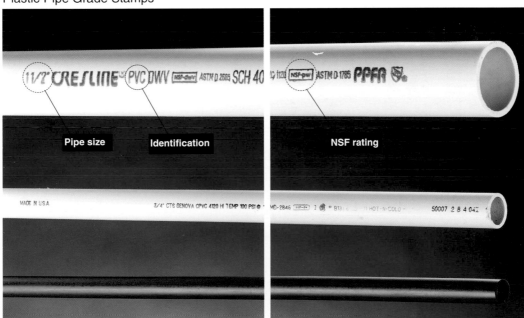

Plastic pipe comes with three important labels. Material identification shows the type of plastic. For sink traps and drain pipes, use PVC pipe. For water supply pipes, use CPVC pipe or PEX. PE is used for outdoor cold water supply. The NSF rating indicates the pipe's proper application. For sink traps and drains, choose PVC pipe that has a "DWV" rating. For water supply pipes, choose CPVC or PEX pipe that has a "PW" (pressurized water) rating. Pipe size is also specified. PVC pipe for drains usually has an inside diameter of 1¼" to 4". CPVC and PEX pipes for water supply usually have an inside diameter of ½" or ¾".

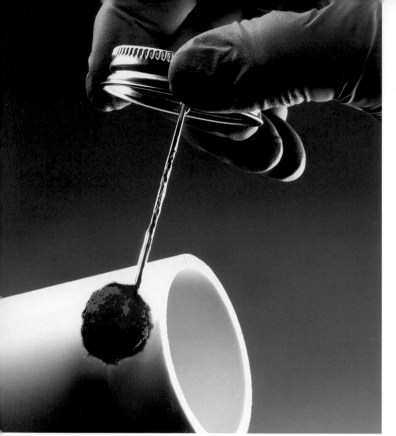

Cutting & Fitting Rigid Plastic Pipe

Cut rigid ABS, PVC, or CPVC plastic pipes with a tubing cutter or with any saw. Cuts must be straight to ensure watertight joints.

Rigid plastics are joined with plastic fittings and solvent glue. Use a solvent glue that is made for the type of plastic pipe you are installing. For example, do not use ABS solvent on PVC pipe. Some solvent glues, called "all-purpose" or "universal" solvents, may be used on all types of plastic pipe.

Solvent glue hardens in about 30 seconds, so test-fit all plastic pipes and fittings before gluing the first joint. For best results, the surfaces of plastic pipes and fittings should be dulled with emery cloth and liquid primer before they are joined.

Liquid solvent glues and primers are toxic and flammable. Provide adequate ventilation when fitting plastics, and store the products away from any source of heat.

Plastic grip fittings can be used to join rigid or flexible plastic pipes to copper plumbing pipes (page 43).

Everything You Need

Tools: tape measure, felt-tipped pen, tubing cutter (or miter box or hacksaw), utility knife, channel-type pliers, gloves.

Materials: plastic pipe, fittings, emery cloth, plastic pipe primer, solvent glue, rag, petroleum jelly.

Specialty materials for plastics include: solvent glues and primer (A), solvent-glue fittings (B), emery cloth (C), and plastic grip fittings (D).

Measuring Plastic Pipe

Find length of plastic pipe needed by measuring between the bottoms of the fitting sockets (fittings shown in cutaway). Mark the length on the pipe with a felt-tipped pen.

How to Cut Rigid Plastic Pipe

Tubing cutter: Tighten tool around pipe so cutting wheel is on marked line. Rotate tool around pipe, tightening screw every two rotations, until pipe snaps.

Miter box: Make straight cuts on all types of plastic pipe with a power or hand miter box.

Hacksaw: Clamp plastic pipe in a portable gripping bench or a vise, and keep the hacksaw blade straight while sawing.

59

How to Solvent-glue Rigid Plastic Pipe

1 Remove rough burrs on cut ends of plastic pipe, using a ulility knife.

Fitting sockets

2 Test-fit all pipes and fittings. Pipes should fit tightly against the bottom of the fitting sockets.

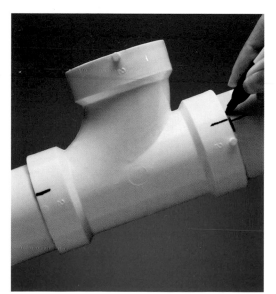

3 Mark depth of the fitting sockets on pipes. Take pipes apart. Clean ends of pipes and fitting sockets with emery cloth.

4 Apply plastic pipe primer to the ends of the pipes and to the insides of the fitting sockets. Primer dulls glossy surfaces and ensures a good seal.

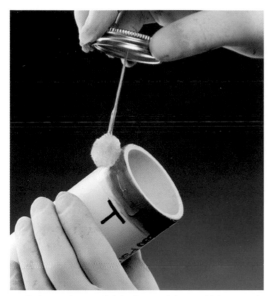

5 Solvent-glue each joint by applying a thick coat of solvent glue to end of pipe. Apply a thin coat of solvent glue to inside surface of fitting socket. Work quickly: solvent glue hardens in about 30 seconds.

6 Quickly position pipe and fitting so that alignment marks are offset by about 2 inches. Force pipe into fitting until the end fits flush against the bottom of the socket.

7 Spread solvent by twisting the pipe until marks are aligned. Hold pipe in place for about 20 seconds to prevent joint from slipping.

8 Wipe away excess solvent glue with a rag. Do not disturb the joint for 30 minutes after gluing.

T-fitting

Female threaded adapter

Barbed PVC male threaded adapter

Valve drain

Hose clamp

PE pipe

Connect PE pipe to an existing cold water supply pipe by splicing in a T-fitting to the copper pipe and attaching a drain-and-waste shutoff valve and a female threaded adapter. Screw a barbed PVC male threaded adapter into the copper fitting, then attach the PE pipe. The drain-and-waste valve allows you to blow the PE line free of water when winterizing the system.

Working with Outdoor Flexible Plastic Pipe

Flexible PE (polyethylene) pipe is used for underground cold water lines. Very inexpensive, PE pipe is commonly used for automatic lawn sprinkler systems and for extending cold water supply to utility sinks in detached garages and sheds.

Unlike other plastics, PE is not solvent-glued, but is joined using "barbed" rigid PVC fittings and stainless steel hose clamps. In cold climates, outdoor plumbing lines should be shut off and drained for winter.

Everything You Need

Tools: tape measure, tubing cutter, screwdriver or wrench.

Materials: flexible pipe, fittings, hose clamps, pipe joint compound.

Connect lengths of PE pipe with a barbed PVC fitting. Secure the connection with stainless steel hose clamps.

How to Cut & Join Outdoor Flexible Plastic Pipe

1 Cut flexible PE pipe with a plastic tubing cutter, or use a miter box or sharp knife. Remove any rough burrs with a utility knife.

2 Fit stainless steel hose clamps over the ends of the flexible pipes being joined.

3 Apply pipe joint compound to the barbed ends of the T-fitting. Work each end of PE pipe over the barbed portions of the fitting and into position.

4 Slide the band clamps over the joint ends. Hand-tighten each clamp with a screwdriver or wrench.

PEX pipe is a relatively new water supply material that's growing in popularity in part because it can be installed with simple mechanical connections.

Working with Cross-linked Polyethylene (PEX)

Cross-linked polyethylene (PEX) is growing quickly in acceptance as a supply pipe for residential plumbing. It's not hard to understand why. Developed in the 1960s but relatively new to the United States, this supply pipe combines the ease of use of flexible tubing with the durability of rigid pipe. It can withstand a wide temperature range (from subfreezing to 180° F); it is inexpensive; and it's quieter than rigid supply pipe.

PEX is flexible plastic (polyethylene, or PE) tubing that's reinforced by a chemical reaction that creates long fibers to increase the strength of the material. It has been allowed by code in Europe and the southern United States for many years but has won approval for residential supply use in most major plumbing codes only recently. It's frequently used in manufactured housing and recreational vehicles and in radiant heating systems. Because it is so flexible, PEX can easily be bent to follow corners and make other changes in direction. From the water main and heater, it is connected into manifold fittings that redistribute the water in much the same manner as a lawn irrigation system.

For standard residential installations, PEX can be joined with very simple fittings and tools. Unions are generally made with a crimping tool and a crimping ring. You simply insert the ends of the pipe you're joining into the ring then clamp down on the ring with the crimping tool. PEX pipe, tools, and fittings can be purchased from most wholesale plumbing suppliers and at many home centers. Coils of PEX are sold in several diameters from ¼" to 1".

Everything You Need

Tools: tape measure, felt-tipped pen, full-circle crimping tool, go/no-go gauge, tubing cutter.

Materials: PEX pipe, manifolds, protector plates, PEX fittings.

Specialty tools for installing PEX are available wherever PEX is sold. The basic set includes a full-circle crimping tool (A), a tubing cutter (B), and a go/no-go gauge (C) to test connections after they've been crimped.

PEX is connected to other water supply materials with transition fittings, including CPVC-to-PEX (A), copper-to-PEX (B), and iron-to-PEX (C).

PEX combines the flexibility of plastic tubing with the durability of rigid supply pipe. It is sold in coils of common supply-pipe diameters.

Tips for Installing PEX Supply Pipe

18"

Do not connect PEX directly to a water heater. Use metal connector tubes.

Check with your local plumbing inspector to verify that PEX is allowed in your municipality. PEX has been endorsed by all major plumbing codes in North America, but your municipality may still be using an older set of codes. Follow the guidelines below when installing PEX:

• Do not install PEX in above-ground exterior applications because it degrades quickly from UV exposure.

• Do not use plastic solvents or petroleum-based products with PEX (they can dissolve the plastic).

• Keep PEX at least 12" away from recessed light fixtures and other potential sources of high heat.

• Do not attach PEX directly to a water heater. Make connections at the heater with metallic tubing (either flexible water-heater connector tubing or rigid copper) at least 18" long; then join it to PEX with a transition fitting.

• Do not install PEX in areas where there is a possibility of mechanical damage or puncture. Always fasten protective plates to wall studs that house PEX.

• Always leave some slack in installed PEX lines to allow for contraction and in case you need to cut off a bad crimp.

• Use the same minimum branch and distribution supply-pipe dimensions for PEX that you'd use for copper or CPVC, according to your local plumbing codes. See page 26 for typical supply-pipe diameters.

Bundle PEX together with plastic ties when running pipe through wall cavities. PEX can contract slightly, so leave some slack in the lines.

1 Cut the pipe to length, making sure to leave enough extra material so the line will have a small amount of slack once the connections are made. A straight, clean cut is very important. For best results, use a tubing cutter.

2 Inspect the cut end to make sure it is clean and smooth. If necessary, deburr the end of the pipe with a sharp utility knife. Slip a crimp ring over the end.

3 Insert the barbed end of the fitting into the pipe until it is snug against the cut edges. Position the crimp ring so it is ⅛" to ¼" from the end of the pipe, covering the barbed end of the fitting. Pinch the fitting to hold it in place.

4 Align the jaws of a full-circle crimping tool over the crimp ring and squeeze the handles together to apply strong, even pressure to the ring.

5 Test the connection to make sure it is mechanically acceptable, using a go/no-go gauge. If the ring does not fit into the gauge properly, cut the pipe near the connection and try again.

How to Plumb a PEX Water-supply System

1 Install copper manifolds (one for hot and one for cold) in an accessible location central to the fixtures. The manifold should have one outlet for each supply line it will support (fixtures that require hot and cold supply will need a separate outlet for each). Run supply lines from the water heater and water main to the copper manifolds. Connect the supply pipes to the manifolds with crimp fittings.

2 A manifold may be attached vertically or horizontally, but it must be anchored with correctly sized hangers screwed to the framing members.

3 Starting at each fixture (and leaving at least 12" of extra pipe exposed), run appropriately sized PEX through holes in the framing to the manifolds. Pipes may be bundled together loosely with plastic ties. Protect the line with a nailing plate at each stud location. Be sure to leave some slack in the supply lines.

4 Support the pipe with a plastic hanger near every floor or ceiling and midway up vertical runs. Also use hangers to guide pipe near the beginnings and ends of curves and near fittings. Use a plastic guide for sharp curves (inset). Do not bend PEX so sharply that it kinks.

5 Cut each branch supply line to length (leave some extra in case you need to recrimp). Install shutoff valves for each outlet (most manifolds come with preattached valves). Connect the PEX branch supply lines to the shutoff valves. Label each pipe. Use a short length of PEX and a plug to seal any unused outlets (inset).

Working with Galvanized Iron

Galvanized iron pipe often is found in older homes, where it is used for water supply and small drain lines. It can be identified by the zinc coating that gives it a silver color and by the threaded fittings used to connect pipes.

Galvanized iron pipes and fittings will corrode with age and eventually must be replaced. Low water pressure may be a sign that the insides of galvanized pipes have a buildup of rust. Blockage usually occurs in elbow fittings. Never try to clean the insides of galvanized iron pipes. Instead, remove and replace them as soon as possible.

Galvanized iron pipe and fittings are available at hardware stores and home improvement centers. Always specify the interior diameter (I.D.) when purchasing galvanized pipes and fittings. Pre-threaded pipes, called *nipples,* are available in lengths from 1" to 1 ft. If you need a longer length, have the store cut and thread the pipe to your dimensions.

Old galvanized iron can be difficult to repair. Fittings often are rusted in place, and what seems like a small job may become a large project. For example, cutting apart a section of pipe to replace a leaky fitting may reveal that adjacent pipes are also in need of replacement. If your job takes an unexpected amount of time, you can cap off any open lines and restore water to the rest of your house. Before you begin a repair, have on hand nipples and end caps that match your pipes.

Taking apart a system of galvanized iron pipes and fittings is time-consuming. Disassembly must start at the end of a pipe run, and each piece must be unscrewed before the next piece can be removed. Reaching the middle of a run to replace a section of pipe can be a long and tedious job. Instead, use a special three-piece fitting called a *union.* A union makes it possible to remove a section of pipe or a fitting without having to take the entire system apart.

NOTE: Galvanized iron is sometimes confused with "black iron." Both types have similar sizes and fittings. Black iron is used only for gas lines.

Everything You Need

Tools: tape measure, reciprocating saw with metal-cutting blade or a hacksaw, pipe wrenches, propane torch, wire brush.

Materials: nipples, end caps, union fitting, pipe joint compound, replacement fittings (if needed).

Measure old pipe. Include ½" at each end for the threaded portion of the pipe inside fitting. Bring overall measurement to the store when shopping for replacement parts.

How to Remove & Replace a Galvanized Iron Pipe

1 Cut through galvanized iron pipe with a reciprocating saw and a metal-cutting blade or with a hacksaw.

2 Hold fitting with one pipe wrench, and use another wrench to remove old pipe. Jaws of wrenches should face opposite directions. Always move wrench handle toward jaw opening.

3 Remove any corroded fittings using two pipe wrenches. With jaws facing in opposite directions, use one wrench to turn fitting and the other to hold the pipe. Clean pipe threads with a wire brush.

4 Heat stubborn fittings with a propane torch to make them easier to remove. Apply flame for 5 to 10 seconds. Protect wood and other flammable materials from heat, using a double layer of sheet metal (page 46).

(continued next page)

5 Replace a section of galvanized iron pipe with a union fitting and two threaded pipes (nipples). When assembled, the union and nipples must equal the length of the pipe that is being replaced.

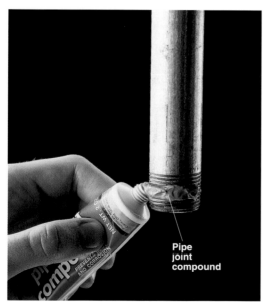

6 Apply a bead of pipe joint compound around threaded ends of all pipes and nipples. Spread compound evenly over threads with fingertip.

7 Screw new fittings onto pipe threads. Tighten fittings with two pipe wrenches, leaving them about ⅛ turn out of alignment to allow assembly of union.

8 Screw first nipple into fitting, and tighten with pipe wrench.

9 Slide ring nut onto the installed nipple, then screw the hubbed union nut onto the nipple and tighten with a pipe wrench.

10 Screw second nipple onto other fitting. Tighten with a pipe wrench.

11 Screw threaded union nut onto second nipple. Tighten with a pipe wrench. Turn pipes into alignment, so that lip of hubbed union nut fits inside threaded union nut.

12 Complete the connection by screwing the ring nut onto the threaded union nut. Tighten ring nut with pipe wrenches.

Working with Cast Iron

Cast iron pipe often is found in older homes, where it is used for large DWV pipes, especially the main stack and sewer service lines. It can be identified by its dark color, rough surface, and large size. Cast iron pipes in home drains usually are 3" or more in diameter.

Cast iron pipes may rust through or hubbed fittings (below) may leak. If your house is more than 30 years old, you may find it necessary to replace a cast iron pipe or joint.

Cast iron is heavy and difficult to cut and fit. For this reason, leaky cast iron pipe usually is replaced with PVC of the same diameter. PVC can be joined to cast iron easily, using a banded coupling (below).

Snap cutters are the traditional tool of choice for cutting cast iron (see page 76), but today's variable-speed reciprocating saws do the job easily and safely. Use a long metal-cutting blade and set the saw at low speed. Wear eye and ear protection when cutting cast iron pipe.

Everything You Need

Tools: tape measure, chalk, adjustable wrenches, reciprocating saw (or rented snap cutter), ratchet wrench, screwdriver.

Materials: riser clamps or strap hangers, two wood blocks, 2½" wallboard screws, banded couplings, plastic replacement pipe.

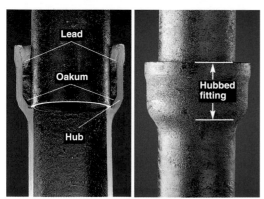

Hubbed fittings (shown cutaway, left) may be used to join old cast iron pipe. Hubbed pipe has a straight end and a flared end. The straight end of one pipe fits inside the hub of the next pipe. Joints are sealed with packing material (oakum) and lead. Repair leaky joints by cutting out the entire hubbed fitting and replacing with plastic pipe.

Banded couplings may be used to replace leaky cast iron with a PVC or ABS plastic pipe. The new plastic pipe is connected to the remaining cast iron pipe with banded coupling. Banded coupling has a neoprene sleeve that seals the joint. Pipes are held together with stainless steel bands and screw clamps.

Strap hangers

Riser clamp

Before cutting a horizontal run of cast iron drain pipe, make sure it is supported with strap hangers every 5 ft. and at every joint connection.

Before cutting a vertical run of cast iron pipe, make sure it is supported at every floor level with a riser clamp. Never cut apart pipe that is not supported.

How to Remove & Replace a Section of Cast Iron Pipe

1 Use chalk to mark cut lines on the cast iron pipe. If replacing a leaky hub, mark at least 6" on each side of hub.

2 Support lower section of pipe by installing a riser clamp flush against bottom plate or floor.

3 Support upper section of pipe by installing a riser clamp 6" above pipe section to be replaced. Attach wood blocks to the studs with 2½" wallboard screws, so that the riser clamp rests on tops of blocks.

(continued next page)

4 Wrap chain of the snap cutter around the pipe, so that the cutting wheels are against the chalk line.

5 Tighten the chain and snap the pipe according to the tool manufacturer's directions.

6 Repeat cutting at the other chalk line. Remove cut section of pipe.

Screw clamp

Banded coupling

Neoprene sleeve

7 Cut a length of PVC plastic pipe to be ½" shorter than the section of cast iron pipe that has been cut away.

8 Slip a banded coupling and a neoprene sleeve onto each end of the cast iron pipe.

9 Make sure the cast iron pipe is seated snugly against the rubber separator ring molded into the interior of the sleeve.

Separator ring

10 Fold back the end of each neoprene sleeve, until the molded separator ring on the inside of the sleeve is visible.

11 Position the new plastic pipe so it is aligned with the cast iron pipes.

12 Roll the ends of the neoprene sleeves over the ends of the new plastic pipe.

13 Slide stainless steel bands and clamps over the neoprene sleeves.

14 Tighten the screw clamps with a ratchet wrench or screwdriver.

New Installation

Installing New Plumbing

A major plumbing project is a complicated affair that often requires demolition and carpentry skills. Bathroom or kitchen plumbing may be unusable for several days while completing the work, so make sure you have a backup bathroom or kitchen space to use during this time.

To ensure that your project goes quickly, always buy plenty of pipe and fittings—at least 25% more than you think you need. Making several extra trips to the building center for last-minute fittings is a nuisance, and it can add many hours to your project. Always purchase from a reputable retailer that will allow you to return leftover fittings for credit.

The how-to projects on the following pages demonstrate standard plumbing techniques but should not be used as a literal blueprint for your own work. Pipe and fitting sizes, fixture layout, and pipe routing will always vary according to individual circumstances. When planning your project, carefully read all the information in the Planning section, especially the material on Understanding Plumbing Codes (pages 24 to 29). Before you begin work, create a detailed plumbing plan to guide your work and help you obtain the required permits. This section includes information on:

- Plumbing Bathrooms (pages 84 to 133)
- Plumbing a Kitchen (pages 134 to 165)
- Miscellaneous Plumbing (pages 166 to 179)

Use 2 × 6 studs to frame "wet walls" when constructing a new bathroom or kitchen. Thicker walls provide more room to run drain pipes and main waste-vent stacks, making installation much easier.

Use masking tape to mark the locations of fixtures and pipes on the walls and floors. Read the layout specifications that come with each sink, tub, or toilet, then mark the drain and supply lines accordingly. Position the fixtures on the floor, and outline them with tape. Measure and adjust until the arrangement is comfortable to you and meets minimum clearance specifications. If you are working in a finished room, prevent damage to wallpaper or paint by using self-adhesive notes to mark the walls.

Consider the location of cabinets when roughing in the water supply and drain stub-outs. You may want to temporarily position the cabinets in their final locations before completing the drain and water supply runs.

Install control valves at the points where the new branch supply lines meet the main distribution pipes. By installing valves, you can continue to supply the rest of the house with water while you are working on the new branches.

(continued next page)

Tips for Installing New Plumbing (continued)

Framing Member	Maximum Hole Size	Maximum Notch Size
2 × 4 loadbearing stud	1⅟₁₆" diameter	⅞" deep
2 × 4 non-loadbearing stud	2½" diameter	1⅟₁₆" deep
2 × 6 loadbearing stud	2¼" diameter	1⅜" deep
2 × 6 non-loadbearing stud	3⅟₁₆" diameter	2⅟₁₆" deep
2 × 6 joists	1½" diameter	⅞" deep
2 × 8 joists	2⅜" diameter	1¼" deep
2 × 10 joists	3⅟₁₆" diameter	1½" deep
2 × 12 joists	3¾" diameter	1⅞" deep

Framing member chart shows the maximum sizes for holes and notches that can be cut into studs and joists when running pipes. Where possible, use notches rather than bored holes, because pipe installation is usually easier. When boring holes, there must be at least ⅝" of wood between the edge of a stud and the hole, and at least 2" between the edge of a joist and the hole. Joists can be notched only in the end ⅓ of the overall span; never in the middle ⅓ of the joist. When two pipes are run through a stud, the pipes should be stacked one over the other, never side by side.

Create access panels so that in the future you will be able to service fixture fittings and shutoff valves located inside the walls. Frame an opening between studs, then trim the opening with wood moldings. Cover the opening with a removable plywood panel the same thickness as the wall surface, then finish it to match the surrounding walls.

Protect pipes from punctures, if they are less than 1¼" from the front face of wall studs or joists, by attaching metal protector plates to the framing members.

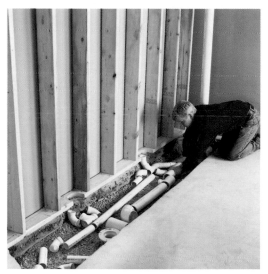

Test-fit materials before solvent-gluing or soldering joints. Test-fitting ensures that you have the correct fittings and enough pipe to do the job, and can help you avoid lengthy delays during installation.

Support pipes adequately. Horizontal and vertical runs of DWV and water supply pipe must be supported at minimum intervals, which are specified by your local plumbing code (page 24). A variety of metal and plastic materials are available for supporting plumbing pipes (page 40).

Use plastic bushings to help hold plumbing pipes securely in holes bored through wall plates, studs, and joists. Bushings can help to cushion the pipes, preventing wear and reducing rattling. Always use manufacturer-recommended bushings with metal wall studs (inset).

Install extra T-fittings on new drain and vent lines so that you can pressure-test the system when the building inspector reviews your installation (page 30). A new DWV line should have these extra T-fittings near the points where the new branch drains and vent pipes reach the main waste-vent stack.

Follow minimum clearance guidelines when planning the locations of bathroom fixtures. Unobstructed access to the fixtures is fundamental to creating a comfortable, safe, and efficient bathroom.

Plumbing Bathrooms

Adding a new bathroom or updating an old one is a sure way to add value to your home. The personal comfort gained from a custom master bathroom can add a new dimension to your relaxation time. And adding a full bath in the basement or a half bath next to the kitchen offers convenience for both family members and guests. When planned and built correctly, a new or remodeled bathroom also improves the resale value of your home.

The first step when planning a bathroom is determining the type of bathroom you want. Do you have your heart set on expanding into a spare bedroom to create the ultimate master bathroom, or do you simply need a functional half bath for convenience? In this section, you'll see three demonstration projects that represent the full range of bathrooms, from a spacious master bathroom to a simple half bath (opposite page).

Next, you'll have to decide on the type of fixtures you need. Visit your local building centers to determine the range of fixtures available and their prices, and visit model homes and remodeling exhibitions to see how professionals arrange and install the fixtures you plan to use.

Once you have determined the scope of your project and settled on a budget, you can develop working plans for your bathroom. When creating a floor plan, always follow minimum clearance guidelines (above), and think about where the drain and water supply pipes will run. You can save yourself many hours of work by positioning fixtures so the pipes can be routed with simple, straight runs rather than with many complicated bends. Make sure that your project complies with local plumbing code regulations for bathroom plumbing.

Master bathroom can include luxury features, such as a large whirlpool tub or multi-jet shower. Our project contains both these features, as well as a pedestal sink and toilet. A spacious bathroom may require substantial construction work if you intend to expand into an adjoining room. See pages 86 to 93.

Basement bathroom is ideal if you have bedrooms or finished recreation areas in your basement. Our project includes a shower, toilet, and pedestal sink. Plumbing a basement bathroom may require that you break into the concrete floor to connect drain pipes. See pages 94 to 99.

Half bath can be easily added to a room that shares a "wet wall" with a kitchen or other bathroom. Our project includes a toilet and pedestal sink. See pages 100 to 101.

1½" vent pipe

1½" vent pipe

1½" vent pipe

1½" vent pipe

1½" drain pipe

1½" drain pipe

3" main waste stack

2" vent pipe

2" drain pipe

Plumbing a Master Bathroom

A large bathroom has more plumbing fixtures and consumes more water than any other room in your house. For this reason, a master bath has special plumbing needs.

Frame bathroom "wet walls" with 2 × 6 studs, to provide plenty of room for running 3" pipes and fittings. If your bathroom includes a heavy whirlpool tub, you will need to strengthen the floor by installing "sister" joists alongside the existing floor joists underneath the tub.

For convenience, our project is divided into the following sequences:

- How to Install DWV Pipes for the Toilet & Sink (pages 87 to 89)
- How to Install DWV Pipes for the Tub & Shower (pages 90 to 91)
- How to Connect the Drain Pipes & Vent Pipes to the Main Waste-Vent Stack (page 92)
- How to Install the Water Supply Pipes (page 93)

Our demonstration bathroom is a second-story master bath. We are installing a 3" vertical drain pipe to service the toilet and the vanity sink, and a 2" vertical pipe to handle the tub and shower drains. The branch drains for the sink and bathtub are 1½" pipes; for the shower, 2" pipe. Each fixture has its own vent pipe extending up into the attic, where they are joined together and connected to the main stack.

1 Use masking tape to outline the locations of the fixtures and pipe runs on the subfloor and walls. Mark the location for a 3" vertical drain pipe on the sole plate in the wall behind the toilet. Mark a 4½"-diameter circle for the toilet drain on the subfloor.

2 Cut out the drain opening for the toilet, using a jig saw. Mark and remove a section of flooring around the toilet area, large enough to provide access for installing the toilet drain and for running drain pipe from the sink. Use a circular saw with blade set to the thickness of the flooring to cut through the subfloor.

3 If a floor joist interferes with the toilet drain, cut away a short section of the joist and box-frame the area with double headers. The framed opening should be just large enough to install the toilet and sink drains.

4 To create a path for the vertical 3" drain pipe, cut a 4½" × 12" notch in the sole plate of the wall behind the toilet. Make a similar cutout in the double wall plate at the bottom of the joist cavity. From the basement, locate the point directly below the cutout by measuring from a reference point, such as the main waste-vent stack.

5 Mark the location for the 3" drain pipe on the basement ceiling, then drill a 1"-diameter hole up through the center of the marked area. Direct the beam of a bright flashlight up into the hole, then return to the bathroom and look down into the wall cavity. If you can see light, return to the basement and cut a 4½"-diameter hole centered over the test hole.

(continued next page)

Low-heel vent 90° fitting

Y-fitting

7 Lower the pipe so the bottom end slides through the opening in the basement ceiling. Support the pipe with vinyl pipe strap wrapped around the low-heel vent 90° fitting and screwed to framing members.

6 Measure and cut a length of 3" drain pipe to reach from the bathroom floor cavity to a point flush with the bottom of the ceiling joists in the basement. Solvent-glue a 3" × 3" × 1½" Y-fitting to the top of the pipe, and a low-heel vent 90° fitting above the Y. The branch inlet on the Y should face toward the sink location; the front inlet on the low-heel should face forward. Carefully lower the pipe into the wall cavity.

8 Use a length of 3" pipe and a 4" × 3" reducing elbow to extend the drain out to the toilet location. Make sure the drain slopes at least ¼" per foot toward the wall, then support it with pipe strap attached to the joists. Insert a short length of pipe into the elbow, so it extends at least 2" above the subfloor. After the new drains are pressure tested, this stub-out will be cut flush with the subfloor and fitted with a toilet flange.

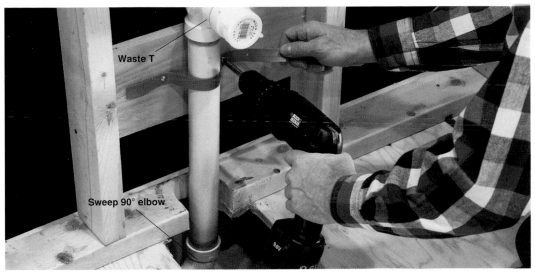

Waste T

Sweep 90° elbow

9 Notch out the sole plate and subfloor below the sink location. Cut a length of 1½" plastic drain pipe, then solvent-glue a waste T to the top of the pipe and a sweep 90° elbow to the bottom. NOTE: The distance from the subfloor to the center of the waste T should be 14" to 18".

The branch of the T should face out, and the discharge on the elbow should face toward the toilet location. Adjust the pipe so the top edge of the elbow nearly touches the bottom of the sole plate. Anchor it with a ¾"-thick backing board nailed between the studs.

10 Dry-fit lengths of 1½" drain pipe and elbows to extend the sink drain to the 3" drain pipe behind the toilet. Use a right-angle drill to bore holes in joists, if needed. Make sure the horizontal drain pipe slopes at least ¼" per foot toward the vertical drain. When satisfied with the layout, solvent-glue the pieces together and support the drain pipe with vinyl pipe straps attached to the joists.

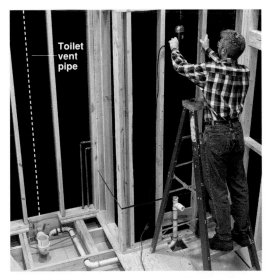

Toilet vent pipe

11 In the top plates of the walls behind the sink and toilet, bore ½"-diameter holes up into the attic. Insert pencils or dowels into the holes, and tape them in place. Enter the attic and locate the pencils, then clear away insulation and cut 2"-diameter holes for the vertical vent pipes. Cut and install 1½" vent pipes running from the toilet and sink drain at least 1 ft. up into the attic.

How to Install DWV Pipes for the Tub & Shower

1 On the subfloor, use masking tape to mark the locations of the tub and shower, the water supply pipes, and the tub and shower drains, according to your plumbing plan. Use a jig saw to cut out a 12"-square opening for each drain, and drill 1"-diameter holes in the subfloor for each water supply riser.

2 When installing a large whirlpool tub, cut away the subfloor to expose the full length of the joists under the tub, then screw or bolt a second joist, called a *sister,* against each existing joist. Make sure both ends of each joist are supported by loadbearing walls.

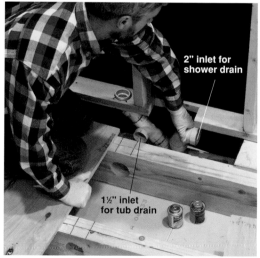

2" inlet for shower drain

1½" inlet for tub drain

3 In a wall adjacent to the tub, establish a route for a 2" vertical waste-vent pipe running from basement to attic. This pipe should be no more than 3½ ft. from the bathtub trap. Then, mark a route for the horizontal drain pipe running from the bathtub drain to the waste-vent pipe location. Cut 3"-diameter holes through the centers of the joists for the bathtub drain.

4 Cut and install a vertical 2" drain pipe running from basement to the joist cavity adjoining the tub location, using the same technique as for the toilet drain (steps 4 to 6, pages 87 to 88). At the top of the drain pipe, use assorted fittings to create three inlets: branch inlets for the bathtub and shower drains and a 1½" top inlet for a vent pipe running to the attic.

5 Dry-fit a 1½" drain pipe running from the bathtub drain location to the vertical waste-vent pipe in the wall. Make sure the pipe slopes ¼" per foot toward the wall. When satisfied with the layout, solvent-glue the pieces together and support the pipe with vinyl pipe straps attached to the joists.

6 Dry-fit a 2" drain pipe from the shower drain to the vertical waste-vent pipe near the tub. Install a solvent-glued trap at the drain location, cut a hole in the sole plate, and insert a 2" × 2" × 1½" vent T within 5 ft. of the trap. Make sure the drain is sloped ¼" per foot downward away from the shower drain. When satisfied with the layout, solvent-glue the pipes together.

7 Cut and install vertical vent pipes for the bathtub and shower, extending up through the wall plates and at least 1 ft. into the attic. These vent pipes will be connected in the attic to the main waste-vent stack. In our project, the shower vent is a 2" pipe, while the bathtub vent is a 1½" pipe.

How to Connect the Drain Pipes to the Main Waste-Vent Stack

1 In the basement, cut into the main waste-vent stack and install the fittings necessary to connect the 3" toilet-sink drain and the 2" bathtub-shower drain. In our project, we created an assembly made of a waste T-fitting with an extra side inlet and two short lengths of pipe, then inserted it into the existing waste-vent stack using banded couplings (pages 76 to 77). Make sure the T-fittings are positioned so the drain pipes will have the proper downward slope toward the stack.

2 Dry-fit Y-fittings with 45° elbows onto the vertical 3" and 2" drain pipes. Position the horizontal drain pipes against the fittings, and mark them for cutting. When satisfied with the layout, solvent-glue the pipes together, then support the pipes every 4 ft. with vinyl pipe straps. Solvent-glue cleanout plugs on the open inlets on the Y-fittings.

How to Connect the Vent Pipes to the Main Waste-Vent Stack

1 In the attic, cut into the main waste-vent stack and install a vent T-fitting, using banded couplings. The side outlet on the vent T should face the new 2" vent pipe running down to the bathroom. Attach a test T-fitting to the vent T. NOTE: If your stack is cast iron, make sure to adequately support it before cutting into it (page 75).

2 Use elbows, vent T-fittings, reducers, and lengths of pipe as needed to link the new vent pipes to the test T-fitting on the main waste-vent stack. Vent pipes can be routed in many ways, but you should make sure the pipes have a slight downward angle to prevent moisture from collecting in the pipes. Support the pipes every 4 ft.

How to Install the Water Supply Pipes

1 After shutting off the water, cut into existing supply pipes and install T-fittings for new branch lines. Notch out studs and run copper pipes to the toilet and sink locations. Use an elbow and threaded female fitting to form the toilet stub-out. Once satisfied with the layout, solder the pipes in place.

2 Cut 1" × 4"-high notches around the wall, and extend the supply pipes to the sink location. Install reducing T-fittings and female threaded fittings for the sink faucet stub-outs. The stub-outs should be positioned about 18" above the floor, spaced 8" apart. Once satisfied with the layout, solder the joints, then insert ¾" blocking behind the stub-outs and strap them in place.

3 Extend the water supply pipes to the bathtub and shower. In our project, we removed the subfloor and notched the joists to run ¾" supply pipes from the sink to a whirlpool bathtub, then to the shower. At the bathtub, we used reducing T-fittings and elbows to create ½" risers for the tub faucet. Solder caps onto the risers; after the subfloor is replaced, the caps will be removed and replaced with shutoff valves.

4 At the shower location, use elbows to create vertical risers where the shower wet wall will be constructed. The risers should extend at least 6" above floor level. Support the risers with a ¾" backer board attached between joists. Solder caps onto the risers. After the shower stall is constructed, the caps will be removed and replaced with shutoff valves.

Vent pipes

Drain pipes

Main stack

Our demonstration bathroom includes a shower, toilet, and pedestal sink arranged in a line to simplify trenching. A 2" drain pipe services the new shower and sink; a 3" pipe services the new toilet. The drain pipes converge at a Y-fitting joined to the existing main drain. The toilet and sink have individual vent pipes that meet inside the wet wall before extending up into the attic, where they join the main waste-vent stack.

Plumbing a Basement Bath

When installing a basement bath, make sure you allow extra time for tearing out the concrete floor to accommodate the drains, and for construction of a wet wall to enclose supply and vent pipes. Constructing your wet wall with 2 × 6 studs and plates will provide ample room for running pipes. Be sure to schedule an inspection by a building official before you replace the concrete and cover the walls with wallboard.

Whenever possible, try to hold down costs by locating your basement bath close to existing drains and supply pipes.

1 Outline a 24"-wide trench on the concrete where new branch drains will run to the main drain. In our project, we ran the trench parallel to an outside wall, leaving a 6" ledge for framing a wet wall. Use a masonry chisel and hand maul to break up concrete near the stack.

2 Use a circular saw and masonry blade to cut along the outline, then break the rest of the trench into convenient chunks with a jackhammer. Remove any remaining concrete with a chisel. Excavate the trench to a depth about 2" deeper than the main drain. At vent locations for the shower and toilet, cut 3" notches in the concrete all the way to the wall.

3 Cut the 2 × 6 framing for the wet wall that will hold the pipes. Cut 3" notches in the bottom plate for the pipes, then secure the plate to the floor with construction adhesive and masonry nails. Install the top plate, then attach studs.

4 Assemble a 2" horizontal drain pipe for the sink and shower, and a 3" drain pipe for the toilet. The 2" drain pipe includes a solvent-glued trap for the shower, a vent T, and a waste Y with 45° elbow for the sink drain. The toilet drain includes a toilet bend and a vent T. Use elbows and straight lengths of pipe to extend the vent and drain pipes to the wet wall. Make sure the vent fittings angle upward from the drain pipe at least 45°.

(continued next page)

5 Use pairs of stakes with vinyl support straps slung between them to cradle drain pipes in the proper position (inset). The drain pipes should be positioned so they slope ¼" per foot down toward the main drain.

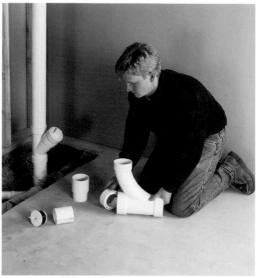

6 Assemble the fittings required to tie the new branch drains into the main drain. In our project, we will be cutting out the cleanout and sweep on the main waste-vent stack in order to install a new assembly that includes a Y-fitting to accept the two new drain pipes.

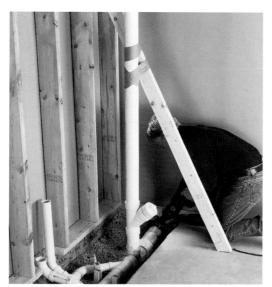

7 Support the main waste-vent stack before cutting. Use a 2 × 4 for a plastic stack, or riser clamps (page 75) for a cast iron stack. Using a reciprocating saw (or a snap cutter), cut into the main drain as close as possible to the stack.

8 Cut into the stack above the cleanout and remove the pipe and fittings. Wear rubber gloves, and have a bucket and plastic bags ready, as old pipes and fittings may be coated with messy sludge.

3" × 3" × 2" reducing Y

9 Test-fit, then solvent-glue the new cleanout and reducing Y assembly into the main drain. Support the weight of the stack by adding sand underneath the Y, but leave plenty of space around the end for connecting the new branch pipes.

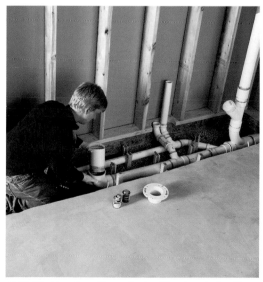

10 Working from the reducing Y, solvent-glue the new drain pipes together. Be careful to maintain proper slope of the drain pipes when gluing. Be sure the toilet and shower drains extend at least 2" above the floor level.

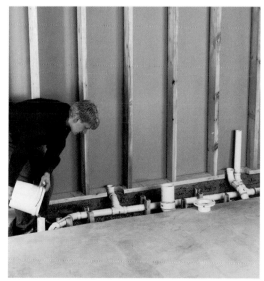

11 Check for leaks by pouring fresh water into each new drain pipe. If no leaks appear, cap or plug the drains with rags to prevent sewer gas from leaking into the work area as you complete the installation.

(continued next page)

12 Run 2" vent pipes from the drains up the inside of the wet wall. Notch the studs and insert a horizontal vent pipe, then attach the vertical vent pipes with an elbow and vent T-fitting. Test-fit all pipes, then solvent-glue them in place.

13 Route the vent pipe from the wet wall to a point below a wall cavity running from the basement to the attic. NOTE: If there is an existing vent pipe in the basement, you can tie into this pipe rather than run the vent to the attic.

14 If you are running vent pipes in a two-story home, remove sections of wall surface as needed to bore holes for running the vent pipe through wall plates. Feed the vent pipe up into the wall cavity from the basement.

15 Wedge the vent pipe in place while you solvent-glue the fittings. Support the vent pipe at each floor with vinyl pipe straps. Do not patch the walls until your work has been inspected by a building official.

16 Cut into the main stack in the attic, and install a vent T-fitting. (If the stack is cast iron use banded couplings, and make sure to support it adequately above and below the cuts.) Attach a test T-fitting to the vent T, then join the new vent pipe to the stack, using elbows and lengths of straight pipe as needed.

17 Shut off the main water supply, cut into the water supply pipes as near as possible to the new bathroom, and install T-fittings. Install full-bore control valves on each line, then run ¾" branch supply pipes down into the wet wall by notching the top wall plate. Extend the pipes across the wall by notching the studs.

18 Use reducing T-fittings to run ½" supplies to each fixture, ending with female threaded adapters. Install backing boards, and strap the pipes in place. Attach metal protector plates over notched studs to protect pipes. After having your work approved by a building official, fill in around the pipes with dirt or sand, then mix and pour new concrete to cover the trench. Trowel the surface smooth, and let the concrete cure for 3 days before installing fixtures.

Vent pipe

Main vent stack

Drain pipe

Plumbing a Half Bath

A first-story half bath is easy to install when located behind a kitchen or existing bathroom, because you can take advantage of accessible supply and DWV lines. It is possible to add a half bath on an upper story or in a location distant from existing plumbing, but the complexity and cost of the project may be increased considerably.

Be sure that the new fixtures are adequately vented. We vented the pedestal sink with a pipe that runs up the wall a few feet before turning to join the main stack. However, if there are higher fixtures draining into the main stack, you would be required to run the vent up to a point at least 6" above the highest fixture before splicing it into the main stack or an existing vent pipe. When the toilet is located within 6 ft. of the stack, as in our design, it requires no additional vent pipe.

The techniques for plumbing a half bath are similar to those used for a master bathroom. Refer to pages 86 to 93 for more detailed information.

In our half bath, the toilet and sink are close to the main stack for ease of installation, but are spaced far enough apart to meet minimum allowed distances between fixtures. Check your local code for any restrictions in your area. Generally, there should be at least 15" from the center of the toilet drain to a side wall or fixture, and a minimum of 21" of space between the front edge of the toilet and the wall.

1 Locate the main waste-vent stack in the wet wall, and remove the wall surface behind the planned location for the toilet and sink. Cut a 4½"-diameter hole for the toilet flange (centered 12" from the wall, for most toilets). Drill two ¾" holes through the sole plate for sink supply lines and one hole for the toilet supply line. Drill a 2" hole for the sink drain.

2 In the basement, cut away a section of the stack and insert two waste T-fittings. The top fitting should have a 3" side inlet for the toilet drain; the bottom fitting requires a 1½" reducing bushing for the sink drain. Install a closet bend and 3" drain pipe for the toilet, and install a 1½" drain pipe with a sweep elbow for the sink.

3 Tap into water distribution pipes with ¾" × ½" reducing T-fittings, then run ½" copper supply pipes through the holes in the sole plate to the sink and toilet. Support all pipes at 4-ft. intervals with strapping attached to joists.

4 Attach drop ear elbows to the ends of the supply pipes, and anchor them to blocking installed between studs. Anchor the drain pipe to the blocking, then run a vertical vent pipe from the waste T-fitting up the wall to a point at least 6" above the highest fixture on the main stack. Then, route the vent pipe horizontally and splice it into the vent stack with a vent T.

Select the shower, bathtub, or whirlpool first when planning your new bathroom. These fixtures, available in a limited range of colors and styles, set the tone for an entire room. Sinks, cabinets, tile, and accessories are available in many styles and colors and can be matched easily to a new tub or whirlpool.

Installing Showers, Bathtubs, & Whirlpools

Installing and hooking up plumbing for bathtubs and showers is a fairly simple job. Whirlpools are more complicated because they also require electrical hookups.

The most difficult task when installing tubs, showers, and whirlpools is moving these bulky fixtures up stairways and through narrow doorways. With a two-wheel dolly and a little help, however, the job is much easier. Measure your doorways and hallways to make sure that any large fixture you buy will fit through them.

If you do not plan to remove and replace your wall surfaces, you still should cut away at least 6" of wall surface above the tub or whirlpool, allowing easier access for installing fixtures.

This section shows:

- Installing showers (pages 104 to 109)
- Installing bathtubs (pages 110 to 115)
- Installing a tub surround (page 115)
- Installing whirlpools (pages 116 to 121)

Left hand

Right hand

Choose the correct tub for your plumbing setup. Alcove-installed tubs with only one side apron are sold as either "left-hand" or "right-hand" models, depending on the location of the predrilled drain and overflow holes in the tub. To determine which type you need, face into the alcove and check whether the tub drain is on your right or your left.

Cross beam

Sister joist

Original joist

3" lag screw

Temporary support post

Install extra floor support if the floor joists below the planned bathtub or whirlpool location are too small, or spaced too far apart. Generally, you should attach additional "sister" joists under the tub area if your current joists are 2 × 10 or smaller, or if they are more than 16" apart. If you are unsure about structural support issues, contact a building inspector or a professional contractor.

Add fiberglass insulation around the body of a bathtub to reduce noise and conserve heat. Before setting the tub in position, wrap unfaced batting around the tub, and secure it with string or twine. For showers and deck-mounted whirlpools, insulate between framing members.

Chisel out mortar around plumbing stub-outs set into basement floors, to make room for drain fittings that slip over the drain pipe. Use a hand maul and masonry chisel, directing the blows away from the pipe, until you have exposed the pipe about 1" below floor level. Wear eye protection.

Installing Showers

Use prefabricated shower panels and a plastic shower base to build an inexpensive, easy-to-install shower stall. For an elegant look and greater durability, you may prefer a custom-tiled shower stall.

Building code requires that each home have a tub in at least one bathroom, but in spare bathrooms or guest baths, you can replace the tub with a shower stall to create space for storage or a second sink.

Most codes also require that showers and combination tub-showers have faucets with anti-scald valves (see below).

Everything You Need

Tools: marker, level, channel-type pliers, hacksaw, hole saw, drill, caulk gun.

Materials: 2 × 4, 1 × 4 lumber, 10d nails, pipe straps, shower pipes & fittings, thin-set mortar, soap, wood screws, wallboard screws, panel adhesive, carpet scrap, tub & tile caulk.

Ceramic tile for custom showers is installed the same way as ceramic wall tile. Ceramic shower accessories are mortared in place during the tile installation.

Anti-scald Valves

Anti-scald valves are safety devices that protect against sudden water temperature changes. They are required by most codes for faucets in showers and combination tub-showers. Once installed, faucets with anti-scald valves look like standard faucets.

Anatomy of a Shower

Shower stalls are available in many different sizes and styles, but the basic elements are the same. Most shower stalls have a supply system, a drain system, and a framed shower alcove.

Shower alcove: A layer of mortar is applied to the subfloor to create a bed for the shower base. Water-resistant wallboard or cementboard is attached to the stall framing members to provide a surface for gluing shower panels.

The supply system: The shower head and shower arm extend out from the wall, where they are connected to the shower pipe with an elbow fitting. The shower pipe rises up from the faucet body, which is supplied by hot and cold supply pipes, and is controlled by a faucet handle and shutoff valves.

The drain system: The drain cover attaches to the drain tailpiece. A rubber gasket on the tailpiece slips over the drain pipe, leading to the P-trap and the branch drain.

Elbow

Shower arm

Shower head

Cross brace for shower head (72" minimum)

Shower framing members

Shower pipe

Faucet body

Water-resistant wallboard

72"

Escutcheon

Faucet handle

Tileboard shower surround

Cross brace for faucet (48")

48"

Shutoff valves

Rubber gasket

Drain tailpiece

Shower base

Drain cover

Mortar base

Drain tailpiece   Subfloor

Drain P-trap

Hot supply pipe   Cold supply pipe   Branch drain

Shower stall shown cutaway for clarity

How to Frame a Shower Alcove

1 Measure shower base and mark its dimensions on the floor. Measure from center of drain pipe to ensure that drain will be centered in the shower alcove. Install blocking between studs in existing walls to provide a surface for anchoring the alcove walls.

2 Build 2 × 4 alcove walls just outside the marked lines on the floor. Anchor the alcove walls to the existing wall and the sub-floor. If necessary, drill holes or cut notches in the sole plate for plumbing pipes.

3 In the stud cavity that will hold the shower faucet and shower head, mark reference points 48" and 72" above the floor to indicate location of the faucet and shower head.

4 Attach 1 × 4 cross braces between studs to provide surfaces for attaching shower head and faucet. Center the cross braces on the marked reference points, and position them flush with the back edge of the studs to provide adequate space for the faucet body (inset) and shower head fittings.

5 Following manufacturer's directions, assemble plumbing pipes and attach faucet body and shower-head fitting to cross braces. (See pages 56 to 69 for information on working with plastic plumbing pipes.) Attach the faucet handle and shower head after the shower panels have been installed (pages 108 to 109).

How to Install a Shower Base

1 Trim the drain pipe in the floor to the height recommended by the manufacturer (usually near or slightly above floor level). Stuff a rag into the drain pipe, and leave it in until you are ready to make the drain connections.

2 Prepare the shower drain piece as directed by the manufacturer, and attach it to the drain opening in the shower base (see inset photo, page 105). Tighten locknut securely onto drain tailpiece to ensure a waterproof fit.

3 Mix a batch of thin-set mortar, then apply a 1" layer to the subfloor, covering the shower base area. Mortar stabilizes and levels the shower base.

4 Apply soap to the outside of the drain pipe in the floor and to the inside of the rubber gasket in the drain tailpiece. Set the shower base onto the drain pipe and press down slowly until the rubber gasket in the drain tailpiece fits snugly over the drain pipe.

5 Press the shower base down into the dry-set mortar, carefully adjusting it so it is level. If directed by manufacturer, anchor the shower base with screws driven through the edge flanges and into the wall studs. Let mortar dry for 6 to 8 hours.

How to Install a Shower Panel Kit

1 Attach the shower dome, if included with the shower panel kit, to the walls of the shower alcove. Refer to the manufacturer's directions for exact installation height for the dome.

2 Screw the mounting strips for the shower door frame to both sides of the shower opening.

3 Make a template for marking pipe hole locations in shower panels, using the panel kit shipping carton or heavy paper. Mark holes for the shower head and the faucet handle(s).

4 Lay the template over the shower panel, and drill out holes with a hole saw. Cut larger holes with a jig saw. For more accurate cuts, use plywood to support the panel near the cutout area.

5 Assemble the shower panels according to manufacturer's directions. Most shower panels are joined together with clips or interlocking flanges before they are installed.

6 Apply heavy beads of panel adhesive to the walls of the shower alcove, and to the mounting strips for the door frame.

7 Slide shower panels into the alcove, and press them against the walls. Pull the panels away from the walls for about 1 minute to let adhesive begin to set, then press the panels back in place.

8 Wedge lengths of scrap lumber between the shower panels to hold the panels in place until the adhesive has set completely. Cover the lumber with scraps of carpeting or rags to avoid damaging the surfaces of the shower panels. Allow the panel adhesive to dry for at least 24 hours before removing the braces.

9 Attach faucet handle(s), shower arm, and shower head (pages 126 to 129), then caulk the seams between the panels and around the base, using tub & tile caulk.

Tub spout nipple

Faucet

Tub ledger

Flashing

Overflow pipe

Shutoff valves

Drain T-fitting

Cold water supply

Drain tailpiece

Branch drain

Hot water supply

P-trap

Wall and floor sections removed for clarity.

The supply system for a bathtub includes hot and cold supply pipes, shutoff valves, a faucet and handle(s), and a spout. Supply connections can be made before or after the tub is installed.

The drain-waste-overflow system for a bathtub includes the overflow pipe, drain T, P-trap, and branch drain. The overflow pipe assembly is attached to the tub before installation.

Installing Bathtubs

Modern plastic polymers and better construction techniques have created a new generation of tubs that are strong, light, and easy to clean. Even if your old fiberglass or cast iron tub is in good condition, consider replacing it with a newer model that resists staining and rusting.

Take care when handling a new bathtub, since the greatest chance of damaging the tub occurs during installation. If the inside of your tub has a protective layer of removable plastic, leave it on during installation. Also set a layer of cardboard into the bottom of the tub for added protection while you work.

Shower pipe connector

Combination tub-showers: Special faucets have a removable plug in the top. Replace the plug with a shower pipe connector.

Everything You Need

Tools: channel-type pliers, hacksaw, carpenter's level, pencil, tape measure, saw, screwdriver, drill, adjustable wrench, trowels.

Materials: tub protector; shims; galvanized deck screws; drain-waste-overflow kit; 1 × 3, 1 × 4, and 2 × 4 lumber; galvanized roofing nails; galvanized roof flashing; thin-set mortar; tub & tile caulk.

Tips for Installing Bathtubs

Drain-waste-overflow kit with stopper mechanism must be purchased separately and attached to the tub before it is installed (pages 112 to 113). Available in both brass and plastic types, most kits include an overflow coverplate, an overflow pipe that can be adjusted to different heights, a drain T-fitting, an adjustable drain tailpiece, and a drain coverplate that screws into the tailpiece.

Build a deck for a drop-in style tub or whirlpool (pages 118 to 119). Used frequently with whirlpools, most decks are finished with cementboard and ceramic tile after the tub or whirlpool is installed.

How to Install a Bathtub in an Alcove

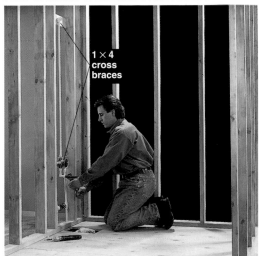

1 Attach the faucet body and showerhead to the water supply pipes, and attach the assembly to 1 × 4 cross braces before installing the tub. Trim the drain pipe to the height specified by the drain-waste-overflow kit manufacturer.

2 Place a tub-bottom protector, which can be cut from the shipping carton, into the tub. Test-fit the tub by sliding it into the alcove so it rests on the sub-floor, flush against the wall studs.

(continued next page)

3 Check the tub rim with a carpenter's level, and shim below the tub to make it level. Mark the top of the nailing flange at each stud. Remove the bathtub from the alcove.

4 Measure the distance from the top of the nailing flange to the underside of the tub rim (inset), and subtract that amount (usually about 1") from the marks on the wall studs. Draw a line at that point on each wall stud.

5 Cut ledger board strips, and attach them to the wall studs just below the mark for the underside of the tub rim (step 4). You may have to install the boards in sections to make room for any structural braces at the ends of the tub.

6 Adjust the drain-waste-overflow assembly (usually sold as a separate kit) to fit the drain and overflow openings. Attach gaskets and washers as directed by the manufacturer, then position the assembly against the tub drain and overflow openings.

7 Apply a ring of plumber's putty to the bottom of the drain piece flange, then insert the drain piece through the drain hole in the bathtub. Screw the drain piece into the drain tailpiece, and tighten until snug. Insert pop-up drain plug.

8 Insert drain plug linkage into the overflow opening, and attach the overflow coverplate with long screws driven into the mounting flange on the overflow pipe. Adjust drain plug linkage as directed by manufacturer.

9 Apply a ½"-thick layer of thin-set mortar to the subfloor with a ½" square-notch trowel, covering the entire area where the tub will rest.

10 Lay soaped 1 × 4 runners across the alcove so they rest on the far sill plate. The runners will allow you to slide the tub into the alcove without disturbing the mortar base.

(continued next page)

11 Slide the tub over the runners and into position, then remove the runners, allowing the tub to settle into the mortar. Press down evenly on the tub rims until they touch the ledger boards.

12 Before mortar sets, nail the tub rim flanges to the wall studs. Rim flanges are attached either by predrilling holes into the flanges and nailing with galvanized roofing nails (top), or by driving roofing nails into studs so the head of the nail covers the rim flange (bottom). After rim flanges are secured, allow the mortar to dry for 6 to 8 hours.

Overflow pipe
Drain tailpiece
Branch drain
Slip nut
P-trap
Floor and sill plate shown cutaway

13 Attach 4"-wide strips of galvanized metal roof flashing over the tub flange to help keep water out of the wall. Leave a ¼" expansion gap between the flashing and the tub rim. Nail the flashing to each wall stud, using 1" galvanized roofing nails.

14 Adjust the drain tailpiece so it will fit into the P-trap (you may have to trim it with a hacksaw), then connect it, using a slip nut. Install wall surfaces, then install faucet handle(s) and tub spout (pages 126 to 129). Finally, caulk all around the bathtub.

How to Install a Tub Surround

1 Mark a cardboard template for the plumbing cutouts, then tape it to the tub surround panel that will cover the plumbing wall. Make the cutouts in the panel with a hole saw or a jig saw.

2 Test-fit surround panels according to manufacturer's suggested installation sequence, and tape them in place. Draw lines along the tops of all the panels, at the outside edges of side panels, and on the tub rim, along the bottoms of panels.

3 Remove panels in reverse order, one at a time. As they are exposed, outline the inside edges of each panel on the surface of the wall.

4 Apply a heavy bead of tub & tile caulk to the tub rim, following the marks made where the panels will rest.

5 Apply panel adhesive recommended by the manufacturer to the wall in the outline area for the first panel. Carefully press the panel in place.

6 Install the rest of the panels in the proper sequence, following the manufacturer's directions for connecting panels and sealing the seams. Press all the panels in place, then brace for drying (page 109, step 8).

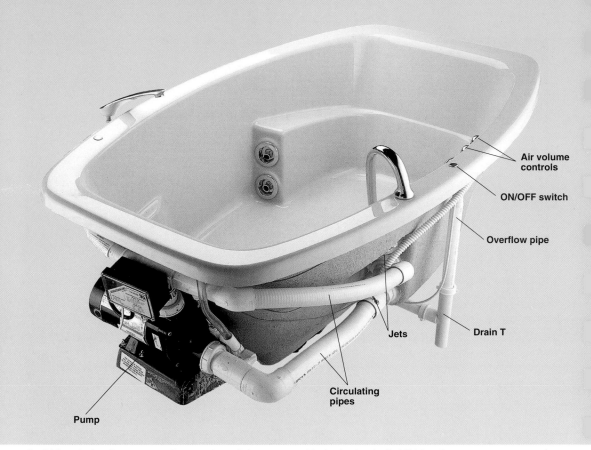

Air volume controls

ON/OFF switch

Overflow pipe

Drain T

Jets

Circulating pipes

Pump

A whirlpool circulates aerated water through jets mounted in the body of tub. Whirlpool pumps move as much as 50 gallons of water per minute to create a relaxing "hydromassage" effect. The pump, pipes, jets, and most of the controls are installed at the factory, making the actual hookup in your home quite simple.

Installing Whirlpools

Installing a whirlpool is very similar to installing a bathtub, once the rough-in is completed. Completing a rough-in for a whirlpool requires that you install a separate electrical circuit for the pump motor. Some building codes specify that a licensed electrician be hired to wire whirlpools; check with your local building inspector.

Select your whirlpool before you do rough-in work, because exact requirements will differ from model to model. Select your faucet to match the trim kit that comes with your whirlpool. When selecting a faucet, make sure the spout is large enough to reach over the tub rim. Most whirlpools use "widespread" faucets because the handles and spout are separate and can be positioned however you like, even on opposite sides of the tub. Most building centers carry flex tube in a variety of lengths for connecting faucet handles and spout.

Everything You Need

Tools: marker, tape measure, circular saw, jig saw, drill & spade bits, hacksaw, screwdriver.

Materials: 2 × 4s, 10d nails, ¾" exterior-grade plywood, deck screws, thin-set mortar, wood spacer blocks, 8-gauge insulated wire, grounding clamp.

Optional Whirlpool Accessories

Air volume controls

Water jet

Overflow coverplate

Mood light

Overflow coverplate

Drain cover

Grab bar

Mood lights are sold as factory-installed accessories by many manufacturers. Most are available with several filters to let you adjust the color to suit your mood. Mood lights are low-voltage fixtures wired through 12-volt transformers. Do not wire mood lights or other accessories into the electrical circuit that supplies the pump motor.

Trim kits for whirlpools are ordered at the time of purchase. Available in a variety of finishes, all of the trim pieces except the grab bar and overflow coverplate normally are installed at the factory.

Requirements for Making Electrical Hookups

5 ft. minimum

Grounding wire

Dedicated 20-amp circuit

MAIN

GFCI circuit breaker

The electrical service for a whirlpool should be a dedicated 115- to 120-volt, 20-amp circuit. The pump motor should be grounded separately, normally to a metal cold water supply pipe. Most whirlpool motors are wired with 12-2 NM cable, but some local codes require the use of conduit. **Remote timer switches** (inset), located at least 5 ft. from the tub, are required by some codes, even for a tub with a built-in timer.

A GFCI circuit breaker at the main service panel is required with whirlpool installations.

How to Install a Whirlpool

1 Outline the planned location of the deck frame on the subfloor. Use the plumbing stub-outs as starting points for measuring. Before you begin to build the deck, check the actual dimensions of your whirlpool tub to make sure they correspond to the dimensions listed in the manufacturer's directions. TIP: Plan your deck so it will be at least 4" wide at all points around the whirlpool.

2 Cut top plates, sill plates, and studs for the deck frame. The height of the frame should allow ¾" for the plywood decking, ¼" for an expansion gap between the deck and the tub rim, and 1" for cementboard, tile, and mortar.

3 Assemble the deck frame. Make sure to leave a framed opening for access panels at the pump location and the drain location. Nail the frame to the floor joists and wall studs or blocking, using 10d nails.

4 Cover the deck frame with ¾" exterior-grade plywood, and attach with screws spaced every 12". Using a template of the whirlpool cutout (usually included with the tub), mark the deck for cutting. If no template is included, make one from the shipping carton. Cutout will be slightly smaller than the outside dimensions of the whirlpool rim.

5 Make the cutout hole in the deck, using a jig saw. Drill a starter hole along the cutout line to start the cut.

6 Measure and mark holes for faucet tailpieces and spout tailpiece according to the faucet manufacturer's suggestions. Drill holes with a spade bit or hole saw.

7 Attach drain-waste-overflow assembly (included with most whirlpools) at the drain and overflow outlets in the tub (pages 112 to 113). Trim the drain pipe in the floor to the proper height.

8 Apply a layer of thin-set mortar to subfloor where tub will rest. Make 12" spacer blocks, 1¼" thick (equal to expansion gap, tile mortar, and cementboard; see step 2). Arrange blocks along the edges of the cutout.

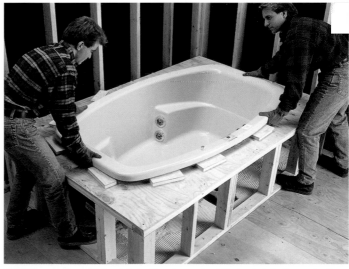

9 With a helper, lift the tub by the rim and set it slowly into the cutout hole. Lower the tub, pressing it into the mortar base, until the rim rests on the spacers at the edges of the cutout area. Avoid moving or shifting the tub once it is in place, and allow the mortar to set for 6 to 8 hours before proceeding with the tub installation. Align the tailpiece of the drain-waste-overflow assembly with the P-trap as you set the tub in place.

(continued next page)

10 Adjust the length of the tailpiece for the drain-waste-overflow assembly, if necessary, then attach assembly to the P-trap in the drain opening, using a slip nut.

11 Inspect the seals on the built-in piping and hoses for loose connections. If you find a problem, contact your dealer for advice. Attempting to fix the problem yourself could void the whirlpool warranty.

12 With power off, remove the wiring cover from the pump motor. Feed circuit wires from the power source or wall timer into the motor. Connect wires according to directions printed on the motor.

13 Attach an insulated 8-gauge wire to the ground lug on the pump motor.

14 Attach the other end of the wire to a metal cold water supply pipe in the wall, using a ground clamp. Test the GFCI circuit breaker.

15 Clean out the tub, then fill it so the water level is at least 3" above the highest water jet.

16 Turn on the pump, and allow it to operate for at least 20 minutes while you check for leaks. Contact your whirlpool dealer if leaks are detected.

17 Staple fiberglass insulation with attached facing to vertical frame supports. Facing should point inward, to keep fibers out of motor. Do not insulate within 6" of pumps, heaters, or lights.

18 Attach cementboard to the sides and top of the deck frame if you plan to install ceramic tile on the deck. Use ¾" plywood for access panel coverings.

19 Attach finish surfaces to deck and deck frame, then install grab bar, faucet, and spout (pages 126 to 129). Fill the joints between the floor and deck, and between the tub rim and deck surface, with tub-and-tile caulk.

Integral sink-countertops are made in standard sizes to fit common vanity widths. Because the sink and countertop are cast from the same material, integral sink-countertops do not leak and do not require extensive caulking and sealing.

Installing Countertops & Sinks

Most bathroom countertops installed today are integral (one-piece) sink-countertop units made from cultured marble or other solid materials, like Corian or Swanstone. Integral sink-countertops are convenient, and many are inexpensive, but style and color options are limited.

Some remodelers and designers still prefer the distinctive look of a custom-built countertop with a self-rimming sink basin, which gives you a much greater selection of styles and colors. Installing a self-rimming sink is very simple.

Pedestal sinks are a third option and are particularly suited for smaller bathrooms.

Everything You Need

Tools: pencil, scissors, carpenter's level, screwdriver, channel-type pliers, ratchet wrench, basin wrench.

Materials: cardboard, masking tape, plumber's putty, lag screws, tub-and-tile caulk.

How to Install an Integral Sink-Countertop

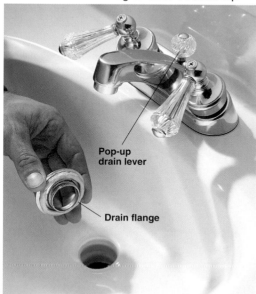

Pop-up drain lever

Drain flange

1 Set the sink-countertop unit onto sawhorses. Attach the faucet (page 126), and slip the drain lever through the faucet body. Place a ring of plumber's putty around the drain flange, then insert the flange in the drain opening.

Sealing gasket

Locknut

Drain tailpiece

Tailpiece extension

2 Thread the locknut and sealing gasket onto the drain tailpiece, then insert the tailpiece into the drain opening and screw it onto the drain flange. Tighten the locknut securely. Attach the tailpiece extension.

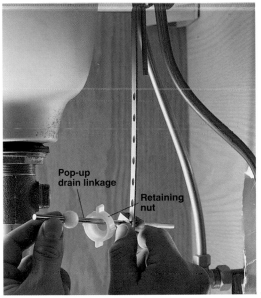

Pop-up drain linkage

Retaining nut

3 Disconnect the pop-up drain linkage from the tail-piece of the sink drain by unscrewing the retaining nut.

4 Apply a layer of tub-and-tile caulk (or adhesive, if specified by the countertop manufacturer) to the top edges of the vanity and to any corner braces.

5 Center the sink-countertop unit over the vanity, so the overhang is equal on both sides and the backsplash of the countertop is flush with the wall. Press the countertop evenly into the caulk.

Cabinets with corner braces: Secure the counter-top to the cabinet by driving a mounting screw through each corner brace and up into the counter-top. NOTE: Cultured marble and other hard counter-tops require predrilling and a plastic screw sleeve.

(continued next page)

How to Install an Integral Sink-Countertop (continued)

6 Attach the drain arm to the drain stub-out in the wall, using a slip nut. Attach one end of the P-trap to the drain arm, and the other to the tailpiece of the sink drain, using slip nuts. Connect supply tubes to the faucet tailpieces (page 127).

7 Seal the gap between the backsplash and the wall with tub-and-tile caulk.

How to Install a Surface-mounted Sink

1 Use a template that is ½" narrower than the sink rim to mark the countertop cutout. Drill a ⅜" starter hole, then use a jig saw to make the cutout. For countertop-mounted faucets, drill holes for the tailpieces, according to the faucet manufacturer's directions.

2 Apply a ring of plumber's putty around the sink cutout. Before setting the sink in place, attach the faucet body to the sink or countertop (page 126), and the drain flange and pop-up drain assembly (page 123, step 3).

3 Set the sink into the cutout area, and gently press the rim of the sink into the plumber's putty. Hook up the drain and supply fittings (step 6, above), then caulk around the sink rim.

How to Install a Pedestal Sink

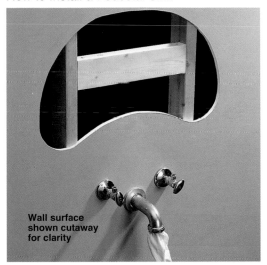

Wall surface shown cutaway for clarity

1 Install 2 × 4 blocking between the wall studs, behind the planned sink location. Cover the wall with water-resistant drywall.

2 Set the basin and pedestal in position, bracing the basin with 2 × 4s. Outline the top of the basin on the wall, and mark the base of the pedestal on the floor. Mark reference points on the wall and floor through the mounting holes found on the back of the sink and the bottom of the pedestal.

3 Set aside the basin and pedestal. Drill pilot holes in the wall and floor at the reference points, then reposition the pedestal. Anchor the pedestal to the floor with lag screws.

4 Attach the faucet (page 126), then set the sink on the pedestal. Align the holes in the back of the sink with the pilot holes drilled in the wall, then drive lag screws and washers into the wall brace, using a ratchet wrench. Do not overtighten the screws.

5 Hook up the drain and supply fittings (page 127). Caulk between the back of the sink and the wall when installation is finished.

Spout
tailpiece

Flex tube

Faucet
valves

Installing Faucets & Spouts

One-piece faucets, with either one or two handles, are the most popular fixtures for bathroom installations.

"Widespread" faucets with separate spout and handles are being installed with increasing frequency, however. Because the handles are connected to the spout with flex tubes that can be 18" or longer, widespread faucets can be arranged in many ways.

Widespread faucets have handles that are installed separately from the spout. Installed most often with whirlpools, widespread faucets also are becoming popular for sinks. The possibilities for arranging widespread faucets are limited only by the length of the flex tubes that connect the faucet handle valves to the spout.

Everything You Need

Tools: drill with spade bit, basin wrench, adjustable wrench, screwdriver.

Materials: plumber's putty, Teflon tape, joint compound.

How to Install a Widespread Faucet

Spout
tailpiece

1 Drill holes for faucet handles and spout in deck or countertop, according to manufacturer's suggestions. Slide a protective washer onto the spout tailpiece, then insert the tailpiece into the spout hole.

Metal
washer

Spout
tailpiece

Locknut

2 From beneath the deck, slide a metal washer onto spout tailpiece, then attach a locknut. Tighten the nut by hand, then check to make sure the spout is properly aligned. Tighten with a basin wrench until snug.

3 Attach faucet valves to deck, using washers and locknuts, as directed by the manufacturer. NOTE: Some widespread faucet valves, like the one above, are inserted up through the hole, and have locknuts above and below.

4 Wrap Teflon tape around spout tailpiece, then attach the connector T to the tailpiece. Attach one end of each flex tube to the T, and the other end to the proper faucet valve.

5 Wrap Teflon tape around faucet valve tailpieces, then attach hot and cold water supply tubes to tailpieces.

6 Attach faucet handle flanges and faucet handles, according to manufacturer's directions. Cover exposed screw heads with trim caps.

How to Install a One-piece Faucet

1 Apply a ring of plumber's putty around the base of the faucet body. (Some faucets use a gasket that does not require plumber's putty—read the manufacturer's directions carefully.)

2 Insert the faucet tailpieces through holes in countertop or sink. From below, thread washers and locknuts over the tailpieces, then tighten the locknuts with a basin wrench until snug.

3 Wrap Teflon tape around the tailpiece threads, then attach the supply tube couplings and tighten until snug. Connect drain linkage, then attach handles and trim caps.

How to Install Tub & Shower Faucets

Two-handled faucet: Screw handle flanges onto faucet valve stems, then attach handle to stems, using mounting screws. Attach spout (page 129) and trim caps. NOTE: Faucet body is attached before wall surface is installed (page 106).

Single-handled faucet: Open built-in shutoff valves, using a screwdriver, then attach escutcheon plate to faucet body with mounting screws. Attach faucet handle with mounting screw, then attach spout and trim cap. NOTE: Faucet body is attached before wall surface is installed (page 106).

How to Connect Supply Tubes

Connect supply tubes after the sink and faucet body are installed. Tubes should be slightly longer than the distance from the shutoff valves to the faucet tailpieces.

Most tubes have a flared end that fits into the fixture tailpiece. Wrap threads of tailpiece with Teflon tape before attaching tubes.

How to Install a Tub Spout

Connect tub spouts by applying joint compound or Teflon tape to the threaded end of the spout nipple that extends from the wall.

Screw the spout onto the nipple, using a long screw-driver as a lever. Some spouts have a set-screw on the underside that must be tightened.

Installing Toilets

Most toilets in the low-to-moderate price range are two-piece units, with a separate tank and bowl, made of vitreous china. One-piece toilets with integral tank and bowl also are available, but the cost is usually two or three times that of two-piece units.

Code regulations requiring low-flow (1.6 gallons per flush) toilets have been on the books for years. After some initial problems with inadequate flush force, manufacturers have re-engineered the toilet traps and flush mechanisms to maximize efficiency. These new models work considerably better than first-generation low-flow toilets from 1980s to mid '90s. Most are reasonably priced and well worth the cost for eliminating aggravation (and double flushing).

Install a toilet by anchoring the bowl to the floor first, then mounting the tank onto the bowl. China fixtures crack easily, so use care when handling them.

Everything You Need

Tools: adjustable wrench, ratchet wrench, or basin wrench, screwdriver.

Materials: wax ring & sleeve, plumber's putty, floor bolts, tank bolts with rubber washers, seat bolts, and mounting nuts.

How to Install a Toilet

1 Turn the bowl upside down, and place a new wax ring and sleeve onto the toilet horn. Apply a ring of plumber's putty around the bottom edge of the toilet base. Waxless rings (inset) are clean and easy to install and are endorsed by most codes.

2 Position the toilet over the toilet flange so the floor bolts fit through the holes in the base of the toilet. The flange should be clean, and the floor bolts should point straight up.

3 Press down on the toilet bowl to compress the wax ring and plumber's putty. Attach washers and nuts to the floor bolts, and tighten with an adjustable wrench until snug. Do not overtighten. Attach trim caps.

Spud washer

Flush valve   Fill valve

4 Turn the tank upside down and set the spud washer over the tailpiece of the flush valve. Turn tank right-side up. NOTE: With some toilets, you will have to purchase a flush handle, fill valve, and flush valve separately.

5 Set the tank onto the bowl, centering the spud washer over the water inlet opening near the back edge of the bowl.

Rubber washer

Tank bolt

6 Shift the tank gently until the tank bolt holes in the tank are aligned over the tank bolt holes in the bowl flange. Place rubber washers onto tank bolts, then insert the bolts down through the holes in the tank.

Washer

Nut   Tank bolt

7 From beneath the bowl flange, attach washers and nuts to the tank bolts, and tighten with a ratchet wrench or basin wrench until snug. Do not overtighten.

Fill valve tailpiece

Coupling nut

Supply tube

8 Cut a piece of supply tube to fit between the shutoff valve and the toilet tank. Attach the tube to the shutoff valve, then to the fill valve tailpiece. Use an adjustable wrench to tighten coupling nuts until they are snug.

Seat bolt

Mounting nut

9 Mount the toilet seat onto the bowl by tightening the mounting nuts onto the seat bolts from below the seat flange.

An internal grinder in a macerating toilet shreds waste from the toilet, as well as connected sinks, and showers. Then the waste is propelled upward by an impeller and into a drain line connected to the main waste-vent stack.

Macerating Toilets

What do you get if you cross a toilet with a food disposer? It may not be the most pleasant combination to consider, but the answer is a macerating toilet. Based on a grinder-and-pump unit that is installed next to or behind the toilet, a macerating toilet grinds waste finely enough that it can be pumped upward through ¾" pipe and evacuated into your existing DWV system. In the right situation, these recently-approved waste disposal units can be the difference between a quick weekend project and a major remodeling undertaking.

Usually installed in basements because they can serve as "up-flush" toilets, macerating toilets will support a toilet, a sink, and a shower or bathtub. They typically are not set up to service the waste volume produced by dishwashers or washing machines. Some toilets use macerating units that can be placed apart from the toilet and connected with a pipe, but most units connect directly to the back of a rear-discharge toilet. The units have inlets that accept drains from the individual fixtures, which must be elevated to

create a drop of ¼" per ft. from the fixture to the macerating unit. When the unit fills up with wastewater, sensors activate the grinding mechanism, which works in conjunction with a grate that acts as a sieve. From there, the wastewater is propelled by an impeller through a ¾" waste pipe and to a Y-fitting at a drain stack.

To Install a Macerating Toilet

Place the macerating unit in the desired location and make the connections to the 1½"-diameter drain lines from the sink and tub or shower to the inlets on the macerating unit. Also connect the ¾" drain line from the soil stack or a branch drain to the discharge port on the unit (you can use either copper or PVC pipe). The drain line may span up to 12 ft. vertically with some models, and it can be run as far as 150 ft. horizontally if a ¼"-per-foot drop is maintained. Read the instructions carefully to learn the limits for your fixture, as well as how to factor in pressure drops that occur when the line makes a bend.

Sample Installation

A **typical macerating unit** will support a toilet, a sink, and a tub and shower. This diagram shows pipe routes for a typical installation. Check local codes before installing.

Once all connections are made at the macerating unit, place the toilet bowl in front of the unit so that the toilet spigot lines up with the accordion connector on the macerating unit. Mark the location of the toilet bowl's mounting-screw holes. Remove the toilet and drill appropriately sized holes for the toilet's mounting lag screws. Join the toilet to the macerating unit as directed by the manufacturer, and secure the toilet to the floor. The toilet tank connects to the bowl like a standard two-piece toilet (see page 130). The water supply connection to the fill valve is also standard (see page 131). Venting should be provided in accordance with local codes and the manufacturer's instructions.

The macerating unit must be plugged in to a 120-volt GFCI-protected outlet (the outlet should be 40" away from the unit). The unit will not function during a power outage. Do not dispose of paper products (other than toilet paper) in the macerating toilet system. Do not use bleach cakes or other submerged tank-and-bowl cleaning products.

The macerating unit fits between the toilet and the wall and is powered by a 120-volt GFCI outlet.

Island sink

Auxiliary
waste-vent
stack

Auxiliary
waste-vent
stack

Drain pipe

Vent pipe

Plumbing a Kitchen

Plumbing a remodeled kitchen is a relatively easy job if your kitchen includes only a wall sink. If your project includes an island sink, however, the work becomes more complicated.

An island sink poses problems because there is no wall in which to run a vent pipe. An island sink requires either a complicated configuration known as a *loop vent* (see pages 135 and 139 to 143) or a device called an *air admittance valve* (AAV), now approved by most codes (see page 146). An AAV eliminates the need for a loop vent in most island sink installations. Check with the local plumbing inspector before designing an installation with an AAV or a loop vent.

For our demonstration kitchen, we divided the project into three phases:
• How to Install DWV Pipes for a Wall Sink (pages 136 to 138)
• How to Install DWV Pipes for an Island Sink (pages 139 to 143)
• How to Install New Supply Pipes (pages 144 to 145)

Our demonstration kitchen includes a double wall sink and an island sink. The 1½" drain for the wall sink connects to an existing 2" galvanized waste-vent stack; since the trap is within 3½ ft. of the stack, no vent pipe is required. The drain for the island sink uses a loop vent configuration connected to an auxiliary waste-vent stack in the basement.

Tips for Plumbing a Kitchen

Insulate exterior walls if you live in a region with freezing winter temperatures. Where possible, run water supply pipes through the floor or interior partition walls, rather than exterior walls.

Use existing waste-vent stacks to connect the new DWV pipes. In addition to a main waste-vent stack, most homes have one or more auxiliary waste-vent stacks in the kitchen that can be used to connect new DWV pipes.

Loop vent makes it possible to vent a sink when there is no adjacent wall to house the vent pipe. The drain is vented with a loop of pipe that arches up against the countertop and away from the drain before dropping through the floor. The vent pipe then runs horizontally

to an existing vent pipe. In our project, we have tied the island vent to a vent pipe extending up from a basement utility sink. NOTE: Loop vents are subject to local code restrictions. Always consult your building inspector for guidelines on venting an island sink.

How to Install DWV Pipes for a Wall Sink

1 Determine the location of the sink drain by marking the position of the sink and base cabinet on the floor. Mark a point on the floor indicating the position of the sink drain opening. This point will serve as a reference for aligning the sink drain stub-out.

2 Mark a route for the new drain pipe through the studs behind the wall sink cabinet. The drain pipe should angle ¼" per foot down toward the waste-vent stack.

3 Use a right-angle drill and hole saw to bore holes for the drain pipe (page 82). On non-loadbearing studs, such as the cripple studs beneath a window, you can notch the studs with a reciprocating saw to simplify the installation of the drain pipe. If the studs are loadbearing, however, you must thread the run though the bored holes, using couplings to join short lengths of pipe as you create the run.

4 Measure, cut, and dry-fit a horizontal drain pipe to run from the waste-vent stack to the sink drain stub-out. Create the stub-out with a 45° elbow and 6" length of 1½" pipe. NOTE: If the sink trap in your instal- lation will be more than 3½ ft. from the waste-vent pipe, you will have to install a waste T and run a vent pipe up the wall, connecting it to the vent stack at a point at least 6" above the lip of the sink.

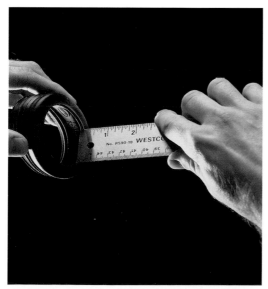

5 Remove the neoprene sleeve from a banded cou- pling, then roll the lip back and measure the thick- ness of the separator ring.

6 Attach two lengths of 2" pipe, at least 4" long, to the top and bottom openings on a 2" × 2" × 1½" waste T. Hold the fitting alongside the waste-vent stack, then mark the stack for cutting, allowing space for the separator rings on the banded couplings.

(continued next page)

7 Use riser clamps and 2 × 4 blocking to support the waste-vent stack above and below the new drain pipe, then cut out the waste-vent stack along the marked lines, using a reciprocating saw and metal-cutting blade.

8 Slide banded couplings onto the cut ends of the waste-vent stack, and roll back the lips of the neoprene sleeves. Position the waste T assembly, then roll the sleeves into place over the plastic pipes.

9 Slide the metal bands into place over the neoprene sleeves, and tighten the clamps with a ratchet wrench or screwdriver.

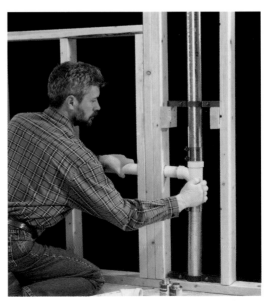

10 Solvent-glue the drain pipe, beginning at the waste-vent stack. Use a 90° elbow and a short length of pipe to create a drain stub-out extending about 4" out from the wall.

How to Install DWV Pipes for an Island Sink

1 Position the base cabinet for the island sink, according to your kitchen plans. Mark the cabinet position on the floor with tape, then move the cabinet out of the way.

2 Create the beginning of the drain and loop vent by test-fitting a drain trap, waste T, two 45° elbows, and a 90° elbow, linking them with 2" lengths of pipe. Measure the width of the loop between the center-points of the fittings.

3 Draw a reference line perpendicular to the wall to use as a guide when positioning the drain pipes. A cardboard template of the sink can help you position the loop vent inside the outline of the cabinet.

4 Position the loop assembly on the floor, and use it as a guide for marking hole locations. Make sure to position the vent loop so the holes are not over joists.

(continued next page)

5 Use a hole saw with a diameter slightly larger than the vent pipes to bore holes in the subfloor at the marked locations. Note the positions of the holes by carefully measuring from the edges of the taped cabinet outline; these measurements will make it easier to position matching holes in the floor of the base cabinet.

6 Reposition the base cabinet, and mark the floor of the cabinet where the drain and vent pipes will run. (Make sure to allow for the thickness of the cabinet sides when measuring.) Use the hole saw to bore holes in the floor of the cabinet, directly above the holes in the subfloor.

7 Measure, cut, and assemble the drain and loop vent assembly. Tape the top of the loop in place against a brace laid across the top of the cabinet, then extend the drain and vent pipes through the holes in the floor of the cabinet. The waste T should be about 18" above the floor, and the drain and vent pipes should extend about 2 ft. through the floor.

8 In the basement, establish a route from the island vent pipe to an existing vent pipe. (In our project, we used the auxiliary waste-vent stack near a utility sink.) Hold a long length of pipe between the pipes, and mark for T-fittings. Cut off the plastic vent pipe at the mark, then dry-fit a waste T-fitting to the end of the pipe.

9 Hold a waste T against the vent stack, and mark the horizontal vent pipe at the correct length. Fit the horizontal pipe into the waste T, then tape the assembly in place against the vent stack. The vent pipe should angle ¼" per foot down toward the drain.

10 Fit a 3" length of pipe in the bottom opening on the T-fitting attached to the vent pipe, then mark both the vent pipe and the drain pipe for 45° elbows. Cut off the drain and vent pipes at the marks, then dry-fit the elbows onto the pipes.

11 Extend both the vent pipe and drain pipe by dry-fitting 3" lengths of pipe and Y-fittings to the elbows. Using a carpenter's level, make sure the horizontal drain pipe will slope toward the waste-vent at a pitch of ¼" per ft. Measure and cut a short length of pipe to fit between the Y-fittings.

(continued next page)

12 Cut a horizontal drain pipe to reach from the vent Y-fitting to the auxiliary waste-vent stack. Attach a waste T to the end of the drain pipe, then position it against the drain stack, maintaining a downward slope of ¼" per ft. Mark the auxiliary stack for cutting above and below the fittings.

13 Cut out the auxiliary stack at the marks. Use the T-fittings and short lengths of pipe to assemble an insert piece to fit between the cutoff ends of the auxiliary stack. The insert assembly should be about ½" shorter than the removed section of stack.

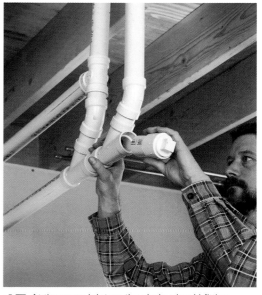

14 Slide banded couplings onto the cut ends of the auxiliary stack, then insert the plastic pipe assembly and loosely tighten the clamps.

15 At the open inlet on the drain pipe Y-fitting, insert a cleanout fitting.

16 Solvent-glue all pipes and fittings found in the basement, beginning with the assembly inserted into the existing waste-vent stack, but do not glue the vertical drain and vent pipes running up into the cabinet. Tighten the banded couplings at the auxiliary stack. Support the horizontal pipes every 4 ft. with strapping nailed to the joists, then detach the vertical pipes extending up into the island cabinet. The final connection for the drain and vent loop will be completed as other phases of the kitchen remodeling project are finished.

17 After installing flooring and attaching cleats for the island base cabinet, cut away the flooring covering the holes for the drain and vent pipes.

18 Install the base cabinet, then insert the drain and vent pipes through the holes in the cabinet floor, and solvent-glue the pieces together.

How to Install New Supply Pipes

1 Drill two 1"-diameter holes, spaced about 6" apart, through the floor of the island base cabinet and the underlying subfloor. Position the holes so they are not over floor joists. Drill similar holes in the floor of the base cabinet for the wall sink.

2 Turn off the water at the main shutoff, and drain the pipes. Cut out any old water supply pipes that obstruct new pipe runs, using a tubing cutter or hacksaw. In our project, we removed the old pipe back to a point where it was convenient to begin the new branch lines.

3 Dry-fit T-fittings on each supply pipe (we used ¾" × ½" × ½" reducing T-fittings). Use elbows and lengths of copper pipe to begin the new branch lines running to the island sink and the wall sink. The parallel pipes should be routed so they are between 3" and 6" apart.

4 Solder the pipes and fittings together, beginning at the T-fittings. Support the horizontal pipe runs with copper pipe straps attached to the joists at least every 6 ft. (Check your local codes for specific strap spacing requirements.)

5 Extend the branch lines to points directly below the holes leading up into the base cabinets. Use elbows and lengths of pipe to form vertical risers extending at least 12" into the base cabinets. Use a small level to position the risers so they are plumb, then mark the pipe for cutting.

6 Fit the horizontal pipes and risers together, and solder them in place. Install blocking between joists, and anchor the risers to the blocking with pipe straps.

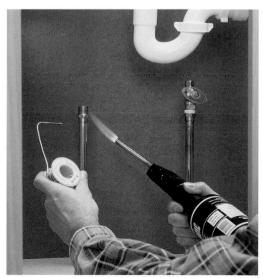

7 Solder male threaded adapters to the tops of the risers, then screw threaded shutoff valves onto the fittings.

Air Admittance Valves

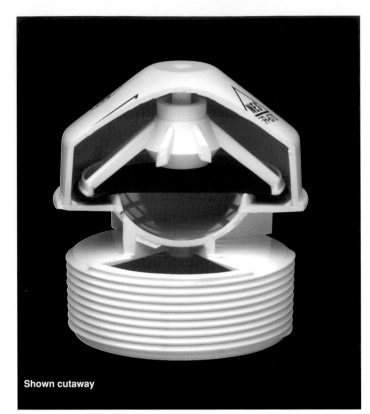

Shown cutaway

Air admittance valves are designed to allow air into the vent system when needed, but to keep it from exiting when the system should remain closed.

The original air admittance valves were spring loaded (right) but advancing technology is replacing these versions with gravity-activated AAVs (left).

The loop vent (page 135) is approved by code in any jurisdiction and is a reliable way to vent your island sink. But in many parts of the country, you'll find another option that is far simpler, if not as time-tested: the air admittance valve (AAV). Invented in the 1970s, AAVs let the necessary amount of air enter a DWV system when water is draining, but they close when the line has emptied to keep sewer gases from escaping.

The advantage of AAVs is that you can install them to vent individual fixtures, reducing the amount of vent piping needed, as well as the number of roof penetrations. You can also install them on branch vent lines to service more than one fixture.

Be sure to check with your local building department before installing them anywhere. Any vent system containing AAVs also must have at least one standard vent outlet to the exterior of the building.

The first AAVs on the market were spring-activated, and you can still purchase these today through wholesale plumbing suppliers or the Internet. Later versions are gravity activated. In these AAVs, the valve is opened by negative line pressure in the drain line created by flushing or draining. When the valve opens, the pressure in the line equalizes.

AAVs can be installed into PVC systems like any other solvent-glued fitting. Always install AAVs according to the manufacturer's specification.

By installing an AAV in a plumbed kitchen island, you can do away with almost all of the complicated loop-vent plumbing. But be sure to check with your local plumbing inspector first. AAVs are allowed in all 50 states but not in some municipalities in selected states.

An AAV connected to the trap of an individual plumbing fixture can eliminate great amounts of vent-plumbing work. In many large public stadiums, for example, each bathroom fixture is vented with an AAV to cut down on the number of long vent runs.

An AAV can be installed on a branch drain servicing as many as six fixtures (check local code), as long as the DWV system has at least one outlet through the roof and outside of the building.

Installing Kitchen Sinks

Standard sinks for kitchens come in numerous bowl configurations, sizes, materials, and mounting styles. When choosing one, start by considering the material. Stainless steel, cast iron, enameled steel, solid surface, and composite are all options, but the vast majority sold today are stainless steel.

Sinks generally mount to countertops in two ways. They can be self-rimming, where the sink rests on top of the countertop, often secured with clamps that hold the sink rim down to the countertop surface, or they can be undermounting, where the sink is screwed into the underside of the countertop (this requires that the edges of

the countertop in the sink area be impervious to water). Most sink manufacturers make models that are designed for undermounting, but if you are reluctant to pay the premium prices charged for true undermount sinks, most self-rimming sinks can be undermounted, too.

Everything You Need

Tools: marker, tape measure, circular saw, jig saw, drill & spade bits, hacksaw, screwdriver.

Materials: 2 × 4s, 10d nails, ¾" exterior-grade plywood, deck screws, dry-set mortar, wood spacer blocks, 8-gauge insulated wire, grounding clamp.

How to Install a Self-rimming Sink

1 After making countertop cutout, lay the sink upside down. Apply a ¼" bead of silicone caulk or plumber's putty around the underside of sink flange.

2 Position front of sink in countertop cutout, by holding it through the drain openings. Carefully lower the sink into position. Press down to create a tight seal, then wipe away excess caulk. Install sink clips (if necessary) and tighten with a screwdriver.

How to Install an Undermount Sink

1 Choose whether you want to have the top edges of the sink flange exposed within the perimeter of the sink cutout in the countertop (A); flush with the edges of the cutout (B); or recessed behind the edges (C).

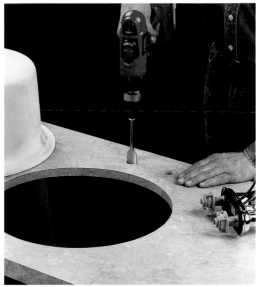

2 Mark the sink opening on the coutertop and make the cutout for the sink. Follow the manufacturer's instructions for cutting your countertop material. Drill holes for the faucet according to manufacturer's specifications.

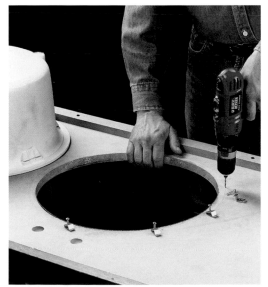

3 Attach the undermount clips to the underside of the countertop, next to the sink cutout.

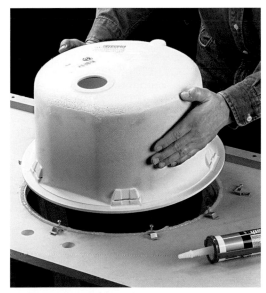

4 Clean the area where the sink will rest on the countertop. Caulk around the edges of the cutout as specified by the sink manufacturer. Then position the sink and tighten the clips.

Installing a Faucet & Drain

Most new kitchen faucets feature single-handle control levers and washerless designs. They rarely require maintenance. More expensive designer styles offer added features, like colorful enameled finishes, detachable spray nozzles, or even digital temperature readouts.

Connect the faucet to hot and cold water lines with easy-to-install flexible supply tubes made from vinyl or braided steel.

Where local codes allow, use plastic piping for drain hookups. Plastic is inexpensive and easy to install. A wide selection of extensions and angle fittings let you easily plumb any sink configuration. Manufacturers offer kits that contain all the fittings needed for attaching a food disposer or dishwasher to the sink drain system.

Everything You Need

Tools: channel-type pliers, hacksaw, basin wrench.

Materials: faucet, flexible vinyl or braided steel supply tubes, drain components.

1 Apply a ¼" bead of plumber's putty or silicone caulk around base of faucet. Apply putty around base of sprayer mount.

2 Insert faucet and sprayer tailpieces into sink openings. Screw mounting nuts onto tailpieces and tighten them securely, using channel-type pliers or basin wrench.

Sprayer base

Faucet base

Tailpiece

Hose stub-out

Tailpiece

Mounting nut

Mounting nut

3 Connect supply tubes to faucet tailpieces, using channel-type pliers. Attach sprayer hose to hose stub-out.

4 Connect left supply tube to the hot water shut-off valve, using channel-type pliers.

5 Attach the right supply tube to the cold water shutoff valve, using channel-type pliers.

Shutoff valves

How to Attach Drain Lines

1 Install sink strainer in each sink drain opening. Apply ¼" bead of plumber's putty around bottom of flange. Insert strainer into drain opening. Place rubber and fiber washers over neck of strainer. Screw locknut onto neck and tighten by tapping nubs with a screwdriver.

2 Attach tailpiece to strainer. Place insert washer in flared end of tailpiece, then attach tailpiece by screwing a slip nut onto sink strainer. If necessary, tailpiece can be cut to fit with a hacksaw.

3 On sinks with two basins, use a continuous waste T-fitting to join the tailpieces (page 152). Attach the fitting with slip washers and nuts. Beveled sides of washers face threaded portions of pipes.

4 Attach the trap arm to the drain stubout, using a slip nut and washer. Beveled side of washer should face threaded drain stub-out. If necessary, trap arm can be cut to fit with a hacksaw.

5 Attach trap bend to trap arm, using slip nuts and washers. Beveled side of washers should face trap bend. Tighten all nuts with channel-type pliers.

New faucet with preattached copper supply tubing: Make water connections by attaching the supply tubing directly to the shutoff valves with compression fittings (page 223).

Kitchen sink with two basins is connected to the drain system by means of a P-trap and continuous waste T-fitting. One end of the continuous waste T connects to the food disposer, the other end to a drain tailpiece running to the other sink basin. Supply tubes controlled by shutoff valves bring water from the hot and cold supply risers to the faucet. The hot water riser may have a supply tube that runs to a dishwasher adjacent to the sink, and the cold water riser may have a saddle valve and tubing running to a refrigerator icemaker.

Strainer

Washers

Locknut

Hot water supply tube

Slip nut

Tailpiece

T-fitting

Hot water shutoff

Trap arm

Beveled washer

Continuous waste T

Trap bend

Copper tubing to icemaker

Air gap

From dishwasher

To sink drain

Dishwasher drain is looped up through an air gap device on the countertop (top), which prevents a plugged sink drain from backing up into the dishwasher. The supply tube running from the hot water supply pipe is connected to the water valve inside the access panel at the bottom of the dishwasher (bottom).

152

Cold water supply tube

Mounting rings

Dishwasher nipple

Braided supply tube to dishwasher

Discharge tube

Cold water shutoff

Food disposer

Dishwasher drain hose

Saddle valve

Installing a Pot Filler

Kitchen design trends are moving ever closer to replicating commercial kitchens in the home. One example of this trend is the pot filler. A long-neck faucet that mounts to the wall behind the cooktop, a pot filler allows you to dispense water directly into large pots on the cooktop. This saves lugging pots of water from the sink to the stove.

Although horizontally mounted models are available, most pot fillers are attached to the wall. Almost all are designed for cold water only. Some have two valves, one at the wall and another at the end of the spout. Other models can be turned on with a foot pedal for safe, hands-free use.

A pot filler will require code-approved supply pipe (½", in most cases) connected with a permanent union at another supply line or the main. The best time to run a new supply is during a remodel. But retrofitting a new supply line and mounting a pot filler is not too difficult as a standalone project. Using PEX supply pipe will make running the new supply line in finished walls easier (see pages 64 to 69 for cutting and fitting PEX).

Everything You Need

Tools: PEX tools, hack saw, reciprocating saw, wallboard tools.

Materials: PEX pipe, pot filler, protector plates, PEX fittings, wallboard patching materials.

Plan the route for the new supply line. In most cases, you will enter the stud cavity of the wall and run a new line directly upward, past the backsplash height of the countertop (A). If the countertop backsplash is removable, avoid wallboard patching by installing the tubing behind the backsplash (B). You may also be able to run the supply line underneath the kitchen if there is an unfinished basement (C).

How to Install a Pot Filler

1 Shut off the water supply and locate the cold water supply riser at the kitchen sink. Cut into the riser and install a T-fitting, or replace the existing shutoff valve on the riser with a multiple-outlet shutoff valve, with an outlet for ½" supply pipe for the pot filler.

2 Plan the route for the new supply line beginning at the T-fitting and working toward the cooktop area (see 154). Determine the height of the new line and then snap chalklines from the sink to the cooktop. With electrical power shut off, remove wall coverings 2" above and below the chalkline and at the location for the pot filler outlet. Make sure the location is high enough to clear your tallest stockpot.

3 Drill ¾" holes in the framing for the supply tubes. Install protector plates if the holes are within 1¼" of the stud edge. Run ½" PEX from the supply riser through the holes to the pot filler location (inset).

4 Attach the new PEX supply line to the T-fitting at the supply riser, installing an accessible shutoff valve on the new line.

5 At the cooktop, install the faucet union as specified by the manufacturer. Add blocking as needed. The pot-filler installed here attaches to a drop-ear L-fitting, mounted to blocking. Apply pipe joint compound to the faucet inlet and thread it on to the L-fitting.

6 Cut and install the wallboard patch. Fit the flange over the inlet. Apply pipe joint compound to the threads of the faucet body. Assemble and adjust the faucet according to the manufacturer's instructions. Test the faucet before refinishing the wallboard.

Upper mounting ring

Sink sleeve

Backup ring

Mounting screw

Dishwasher nipple

Lower mounting ring

Sound insulation

Grinding ring

Discharge opening

Impellers

Drain chamber

Motor

Shown cutaway

A food disposer grinds food waste so it can be flushed away through the sink drain system. A quality disposer has a ½-horsepower, self-reversing motor that will not jam. Other features to look for include foam sound insulation, a cast iron grinding ring, and overload protection that allows the motor to be reset if it overheats. Better food disposers have a 5-year manufacturer's warranty.

Installing a Food Disposer

Choose a food disposer with a motor rated at ½ horsepower or more. Look for a self-reversing feature that prevents the disposer from jamming. Better models carry a manufacturer's warranty of up to five years.

Local plumbing codes may require that a disposer be plugged into a grounded outlet controlled by a switch above the sink.

Everything You Need

Tools: (pages 34 to 37), screwdriver.

Materials: 12-gauge appliance cord with grounded plug, wire connectors.

How to Install a Food Disposer

1 Remove plate on bottom of disposer. Use combination tool to strip about ½" of insulation from each wire in appliance cord. Connect white wires, using a wire connector. Connect black wires. Attach green insulated wire to green ground screw. Gently push wires into opening. Replace bottom plate.

Flange
Sleeve
Fiber gasket
Backup ring
Upper mounting ring
Snap ring

Upper mounting ring
Mounting screw
Lower mounting ring
Mounting lug
Mounting ear

Discharge tube

2 Apply ¼" bead of plumber's putty under the flange of the disposer sink sleeve. Insert sleeve in drain opening, and slip the fiber gasket and the backup ring onto the sleeve. Place upper mounting ring on sleeve and slide snap ring into groove.

3 Tighten the three mounting screws. Hold disposer against upper mounting ring so that the mounting lugs on the lower mounting ring are directly under the mounting screws. Turn the lower mounting ring clockwise until the disposer is supported by the mounting assembly.

4 Attach the discharge tube to the discharge opening on the side of the disposer, using the rubber washer and metal flange.

Dishwasher nipple
Hose clamp

Continuous waste

Mounting lug
Lower mounting ring

5 If dishwasher will be attached, knock out the plug in the dishwasher nipple, using a screwdriver. Attach the dishwasher drain hose to nipple with hose clamp.

6 Attach the discharge tube to the continuous waste pipe with slip washer and nut. If discharge tube is too long, cut it with a hacksaw or tubing cutter.

7 Lock disposer into place. Insert a screwdriver or disposer wrench into a mounting lug on the lower mounting ring, and turn clockwise until the mounting ears are locked. Tighten all drain slip nuts with channel-type pliers.

157

Installing a Dishwasher

A dishwasher requires a hot water supply connection, a drain connection, and an electrical hookup. These connections are easiest to make when the dishwasher is located next to the sink.

Hot water reaches the dishwasher through a supply tube. With a multiple-outlet shutoff valve or brass T-fitting on the hot water pipe, you can control water to the sink and dishwasher with the same valve.

For safety, loop the dishwasher drain hose up through an air gap mounted on the sink or countertop. An air gap prevents a clogged drain from backing up into the dishwasher.

A dishwasher requires its own 20-amp electrical circuit. For convenience, have this circuit wired into one-half of a split duplex receptacle. The other half of the receptacle powers the food disposer.

Everything You Need

Tools: (pages 34 to 37), screwdriver, utility knife, drill with 2" hole saw.

Materials: air gap, drain hose, waste-T tailpiece, braided steel supply tube, rubber connector for food disposer, brass L-fitting, 12-gauge appliance power cord.

How to Install a Dishwasher

1 Mount air gap, using one of the predrilled sink openings. Or, bore a hole in the countertop with a drill and hole saw. Attach the air gap by tightening mounting nut over the tailpiece with channel-type pliers.

2 Cut openings in side of sink base cabinet for electrical and plumbing lines, using a drill and hole saw. Dishwasher instructions specify size and location of openings. Slide dishwasher into place, feeding rubber drain hose through hole in cabinet. Level the dishwasher.

3 Attach the dishwasher drain hose to the smaller, straight nipple on the air gap, using a hose clamp. If hose is too long, cut to correct length with a utility knife. Cut another length of rubber hose to reach from the larger, angled nipple to the food disposer. Attach hose to the air gap and to the nipple on disposer with hose clamps.

On sinks without food disposer, attach a special waste-T sink tailpiece to sink strainer. Attach the drain hose to the waste-T nipple with a hose clamp.

4 Connect dishwasher supply tube to hot water shutoff, using channel-type pliers. This connection is easiest with a multiple-outlet shutoff valve or a brass T-fitting (page 152).

5 Remove access panel on front of dishwasher. Connect a brass L-fitting to the threaded opening on the dishwasher water valve, and tighten with channel-type pliers.

6 Run the dishwasher supply tube from the hot water pipe to the dishwasher water valve. Attach supply tube to L-fitting, using channel-type pliers.

7 Remove cover on electrical box. Run power cord from outlet through to electrical box. Strip about ½" of insulation from each cord wire, using combination tool. Connect black wires, using a wire connector. Connect white wires. Connect green insulated wire to ground screw. Replace box cover and dishwasher access panel. Carefully slide unit into cabinet opening and level adjustable feet.

Connecting a Refrigerator Ice Maker

Many refrigerators come with ice makers, which need to be attached to a water supply. The most difficult aspect is locating a water supply close to the refrigerator. Most installations involve drilling a hole through the floor and attaching the tubing to a nearby supply line in the basement.

Parts for ice-maker installation are available separately, or as kits containing saddle valve, tubing, and compression fittings. Appliance stores, service centers, and home centers have kits available with copper or plastic tubing. The plastic tubing can become brittle over time and possibly break, so most appliance centers recommend using copper tubing.

Saddle valves also present a potential leakage problem, and they are rarely code approved. Many plumbers prefer not to use them. A much better installation is a T-fitting connected to a shutoff valve with a ¼" outlet or dual-outlet shutoff valve (shown on page 159, step 4).

Tools and Materials

Tools: adjustable wrench, drill, propane torch.

Materials: ¼" soft copper tubing, T-fitting and shutoff valve or dual-outlet shutoff valve, brass compression fittings.

Refrigerator ice makers use water from a nearby supply riser to make ice. When improperly installed, ice makers are notorious for leaking.

1 Drill a ⅜" hole through the floor at the back of the refrigerator area. Run ¼" flexible copper supply tubing down through the hole to a nearby cold water supply line. If there is no accessible supply below the refrigerator, route the supply tube to a nearby sink supply riser. Support the tubing with pipe hangers as necessary.

2 Shut off the water at the main shutoff valve. Cut into the cold supply pipe near the hole in the floor. Install a T-fitting. Install a shutoff valve correctly sized for the T-fitting and the ice-maker supply tube. Use techniques described on pages 44 to 50. To attach a saddle valve instead, see page 43.

3 Run copper tubing to refrigerator. Connect water supply tube to the water valve tube, using a ¼" compression elbow. Slide coupling nuts and compression rings over tubes, and insert tubes into elbow. Tighten coupling nuts.

4 Arrange the copper coil so it won't be pinched when the refrigerator is moved back into place. Carefully roll the refrigerator into place and lock the wheels.

Installing a Hot Water Dispenser

Hot water dispensers keep small amounts of drinking water hot so you can brew tea or make instant soup right out of the tap. They're not too expensive ($100 to $300) and are relatively easy to install. Consumer models plug in to a GFCI receptacle. For water, tap into a nearby cold water supply pipe.

Hot water dispensers are also reasonably inexpensive to operate. Manufacturers suggest average use (10 cups) will cost about $.06 a day. This may actually be less than the energy cost of boiling water on a stovetop or in a microwave.

Many models also dispense cold water, and some include an inline reverse-osmosis filter.

If there is an unused fourth opening in the kitchen sink rim (after the faucet and two handles), install the hot water dispenser there. If not, drill a hole (generally 1¼") in the rim of a stainless steel sink rim. Or drill a hole into the countertop near the back rim of the sink.

The dispenser will require a 120-volt GFCI receptacle. Many sink cabinets have a receptacle that supplies a food disposer. You may be able to use the second plug for the hot water dispenser (check local code). If not, install a new circuit with a receptacle in the base cabinet.

Everything You Need

Tools: adjustable wrench, drill, propane torch.

Materials: hot water dispenser, ¼" soft copper tubing, T-fitting and shutoff valve or dual-outlet shutoff valve, brass compression fittings.

Hot water dispensers keep a small amount of water piping hot and ready to use.

How to Install a Hot Water Dispenser

1 Slip the washers for the dispenser onto the faucet stem so the rubber washer will contact the countertop or sink rim. Insert the faucet body into the hole from above.

2 Make sure the faucet's dispenser tubes are straight. Then, with an assistant holding the dispenser head in place above the countertop, position yourself beneath the countertop. Slide the fiber washer over the dispenser tubes and onto the threaded stem. Hand-tighten the dispenser wing nut to secure the dispenser to the countertop or sink rim.

3 Shut off the water at the main. Attach a T-fitting and shutoff valve or a dual-outlet shutoff valve (see page 159) to a water supply riser. Attach the ¼" supply tube from the dispenser body to the outlet at the shutoff valve .

4 Mount the tank on the wall, locating and adjusting the mounting bracket so the tank is level and fastened securely. Do not plug in. Attach the copper supply tubing from the dispenser head to the water inlet on the dispenser tank.

5 Connect the flexible supply tube from the dispenser head to the hot water outlet on the tank. If the dispenser uses a vent tube, connect it as directed by the manufacturer. Turn the water on, and depress the dispenser handle to permit water into the tank. Let the water run and watch for any leaks. Plug the heater unit into a GFCI-protected outlet. Adjust the temperature as desired.

An undersink water filtration system: saddle valve (A), filtration unit (B), T-coupling (C), drinking water faucet (D), and refrigerator icemaker line (E). Additional filters for refrigerator icemakers can be installed (F).

Installing an Undersink Water Filtration System

A point-of-use water filtration system is easily installed underneath the kitchen sink. It provides better-tasting and safer water by reducing lead, chlorine, rust, nitrates/nitrites, and other contaminants.

Though most systems are installed in much the same way, always follow the manufacturer's instructions. Our installation includes a secondary filter that supplies a refrigerator icemaker. If you choose not to install this filter, the main filter is connected directly to the drinking faucet. The drinking faucet included with most units is installed using the same methods as for a standard faucet (page 222).

Everything You Need

Tools: drill, wrenches.

Materials: ¼" flexible vinyl mesh tubing, saddle valve, brass compression fittings, T-valve, point-of-use filtration unit, filters, refrigerator icemaker filter (optional).

How to Install an Undersink Water Filtration System

1 Mount filter unit under sink, according to manufacturer's directions. Shut off main water supply, then install a saddle valve on the cold water line (page 239), making sure the valve is closed. Connect vinyl mesh tubing from intake side of filtration unit to the saddle valve. Attach a vinyl mesh tube to the out-take side of the water filter unit. If you're installing an icemaker filter, attach a T-coupling to the free end of this tube (see photo, top).

2 Install drinking water faucet on countertop, according to manufacturer's directions. Connect a vinyl mesh tube between the faucet tailpiece and the top of the T-coupling (or directly to the water filter, if no icemaker filter is being installed). Attach the icemaker filter to the other outlet on the T-coupling, then run flexible tubing to the icemaker. Turn on water and open saddle valve. Inspect all connections for leaks.

Installing a Whole-house Water Filtration System

A whole-house water filtration system is installed along the supply pipe carrying water to the house, located after the water meter, but before any other appliances in the pipe line. A whole-house system reduces the same elements as an under-sink system and can also help reduce the iron flowing into the water softener, prolonging its life.

Always follow the manufacturer's directions for your particular unit. If your electrical system is grounded through the water pipes, make sure to install ground clamps on both sides of the filtration unit with a connecting jumper wire (page 56). Globe valves (page 239) should be installed within 6" of the intake and the outtake sides of the filter.

Filters must be replaced every few months, depending on type of manufacturer. The filtration unit cover unscrews for filter access.

Everything You Need

Tools: tape measure, pipe cutter, wrenches.

Materials: whole-house filtration unit, filters.

A whole-house water filtration system: intake side (A), supply pipe from the water meter pipe (B), outtake side to the house supply pipe (C), filter (D), and filtration unit cover (E).

How to Install a Whole-House Water Filtration System

1 Shut off main water supply and turn on faucets to drain pipes. Position unit after water meter, but before any other appliances in supply pipe. Measure and mark pipe to accomodate the filtration unit. Cut pipe at marks with a pipe cutter. Join water meter side of pipe with intake side of unit, and house supply side of pipe with outtake side of unit. Tighten with a wrench.

2 Install a filter and screw filtration unit cover to bottom of the filtration unit. Attach a jumper wire to pipes on other side of unit, using pipe clamps (page 56). Open main water supply lines to restore the water supply. Allow faucets to run for a few minutes, as you check to make sure that the system is working properly.

Installing a Whole-house Humidifier

Humidifiers improve the comfort of your home by adding moisture to the air. Typically, whole-house humidifiers are attached to the furnace in forced-air systems and are tied into the water supply and drain systems. Whole-house humidifiers can be manual or automatic. Manual models are cheaper, but they require monitoring of humidity levels and user adjustment. Automatic models have sensors that gauge the amount of humidity in the air and adjust moisture levels accordingly. Unlike earlier models, today's humidifiers distribute water on demand, so you don't need to be concerned about mold growth in the water reservoir.

Most home humidifiers are one of two types: drum-style and drip-style. A drum-style humidifier has a rotating drum fitted with an absorbent filter. The drum rotates and constantly picks up water from a reservoir. Air entering the furnace passes through the drum and carries water vapor into the heating system. A float controls the water level in the reservoir. In a drip-style humidifier, fresh water flows into a distribution tray and trickles through an evaporative pad filter. Any moisture that's not carried away by air flowing through the pad drains into a drain tube.

Drum-style units are generally cheaper but require more maintenance. They use water more efficiently. Either style requires regular inspection.

Some humidifiers are installed on the return-air side of the furnace and humidified unheated air that passes into the furnace, which then heats and distributes it. Other humidifiers direct heated air through the filter by way of a bypass duct,

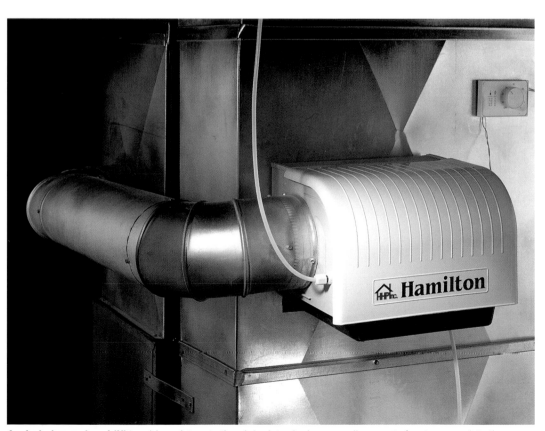

A whole-house humidifier adds moisture to the air by introducing a small amount of water vapor into the forced-air heating and cooling system.

which redirects heated air from the furnace back into the return-air duct to aid in evaporation. A third style employs a fan that runs independently of the furnace blower. This type is installed on the hot-air side of the furnace and does not bypass back to the return-air side.

Installing a whole-house humidifier is a relatively easy task if you have a forced-air heating system. Installation requires tying into the ductwork as well as the water supply and drain systems.

The humidifier unit comes with templates that you attach to the ductwork as guides for making cutouts for the main evaporator unit and the humidistat. The humidistat is an electronic gauge that measures air humidity levels and controls the humidifier output.

Although installing a central humidifier is not difficult, equipment manufacturers prefer that you hire a professional installer for the job. Be aware that choosing to do the work yourself may affect your warranty.

Everything You Need

Tools: aviator's snips, screwdriver, utility knife, drill, adjustable wrenches, felt-tipped pen, gloves.

Materials: whole-house humidifier, vent pipe, sheet metal screws.

Whole-house humidifiers work in existing forced-air duct work. In most installations, the humidifier is installed on the return-air plenum. Heated air from the warm air plenum enters the humidifier through a bypass duct and vaporizes water in the humidifier. The moist air is then distributed through the house.

Drum humidifiers add moisture to the cold air supply before it is heated in the burner. They are inexpensive and water-efficient but have less capacity than other types.

Drip humidifiers disperse water into a pad filter where it is evaporated by heated air directed back into the air supply side via a bypass duct. They waste a significant amount of water but can humidify large spaces.

How to Install a Whole-house Humidifier

1 Turn off the furnace and central air conditioner. Trace the manufacturer's template for the main humidifier unit onto the duct, according to the instructions. If the humidifier is a direct drum or bypass drip model, the main unit is installed on the cold-air side; if it has an independent fan, it is installed on the hot-air side. Drill a starter hole, and then cut the opening for the unit with aviator's snips.

2 Secure the main humidifier unit (or the housing for it, on some models) in the opening with sheet metal screws.

3 If your humidifier unit has a bypass vent, make a cutout for the 6"-dia. vent pipe in the hot-air plenum, according to the manufacturer's specifications.

4 Install a collar in the round cutout, then run vent pipe for the bypass, securing the connections with sheet metal screws.

5 Position and install the humidistat as directed by the manufacturer (normally, it is attached on the cold air plenum near the furnace burner)

6 Connect the humidistat to the furnace. Most humidifiers are connected to the accessory panel on your furnace controls so they automatically turn on whenever the furnace blower cycles on. Note that some humidifiers run off of low-voltage power and may use a transformer to step down the voltage from the accessory panel.

7 Connect the solenoid. Connect the leads from the humidistat to the contacts on the solenoid valve, located on the humidifier unit.

8 Tap into a nearby water supply line (hot is preferable but not essential) with a saddle valve (if local code allows) or a T-fitting. Run supply tubing to the solenoid valve, and connect the supply tubing with a compression fitting. If your humidifier has a drain tube, run it to a drain opening as recommended by the manufacturer. Some units do not have a drain line because they automatically evaporate any excess water into the heating system. Install the filter, and test the system.

Installing a Water Softener

A water softener can improve washing machine and dishwasher performance and lengthen the life of a water heater by removing minerals from water.

A water softener removes minerals from hard water. These minerals can cause scale buildup in plumbing, reducing water flow and potentially damaging your water heater. They also prevent detergents from dissolving, and they can leave residue on dishes and surfaces.

Hard water entering the water softener first flows into a mineral tank that is loaded with negatively-charged plastic beads. When the water passes over the beads, positively-charged magnesium and calcium in the hard water cling to the beads and are replaced in the water by sodium, softening the water. Mineral accumulation eventually reduces the effectiveness of the beads. To recharge the system, the water softener periodically rinses the beads in the mineral tank with salt water from a brine tank.

When the water softener is in recharge mode, hard water bypasses the softener through a bypass valve. Some models have a second mineral tank so soft water supply is ongoing.

The following installation softens all water supplied to the house. As a result, some may notice a change in the water's taste, while others may be concerned about additional sodium intake. To address this, softeners may also be installed so that only hot water is softened (the softener is installed between the main and the water heater). Another option is to run a separate cold drinking water supply to the kitchen or to install an undersink water filter (see page 164) to remove sodium from drinking water.

Everything You Need

Tools: pipe wrenches, hacksaw or tubing cutter, level, propane torch, adjustable wrench.

Materials: wood shims, solder, Teflon tape, ¾" copper pipe and T-fittings, pipe joint compound.

How to Install a Water Softener

1 Install the bypass valve. Position the softener unit and shim as needed to level it.

2 Attach compression unions to both the bypass valve inlet and outlet to connect to the supply line.

3 Connect the water supply. Run supply pipe from the water main to the inlet on the bypass valve. Run supply tubing from the soft water outlet back into the main water supply line. Attach the water supply lines to the bypass valves with compression fittings.

4 Connect the vent tube as specified by the manufacturer. Secure the vent tube at a nearby drain.

5 Connect the overflow tube to the brine tank as directed by the manufacturer. The overflow tube provides a path for water to get out if there is a clog or malfunction in the tank system. Secure the overflow tube at a drain.

6 Connect the inlet and outlet supply risers with a grounding clamp (supplied by the manufacturer) if the electrical system grounds through the water main. Test for leaks and make any electrical connections as directed by the manufacturer.

A washing machine with standpipe drain: washing machine drain hose (A), 2" standpipe drain with trap (B), waste line (C), utility sink drain pipe (D), hot and cold supply lines with hose bibs (E),and rubber supply hoses to washing machine (F).

Installing a Washing Machine Standpipe Drain

Although in many houses the washing machine drain hose is hung loosely over the side of the utility sink, this configuration is frowned upon by building codes. Instead, you should install a standpipe drain that allows the washing machine to drain directly into the utility sink's drain line.

Standpipes with attached P-traps can be purchased at many home centers. A 2"-pipe is required by must building codes. The top of the standpipe should be higher than the highest water level in the washing machine, but not shorter than 34".

Hose bibs are installed in the hot and cold supply lines of the utility sink to provide the water supply to the washing machine.

Everything You Need

Tools: tape measure, reciprocating saw, drill.

Materials: 2" standpipe drain with trap, 2" Y-fitting, waste T-fitting, pipe strap, 2½" deck screws, ½" screws, hose bibs, two rubber supply hoses, Teflon tape.

How to Install a Standpipe Drain

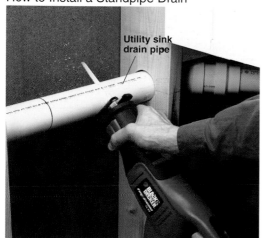

1 Measure and mark the size and location of a waste T-fitting in the drain line. Remove the marked section, using a reciprocating saw. Make cuts as straight as possible.

2 Use a utility knife to remove rough burrs on the cut ends of the pipe. Dry-fit the waste Y-fitting into the drain line to make sure it properly fits, then solvent-glue it in place (pages 58 to 61).

172

3 Dry fit a 90° elbow and a 2" standpipe with trap to the waste Y-fitting. Make sure the standpipe is taller than the highest water level in the washing machine (a minimum of 34"). Solvent-glue all the pipes in place.

4 Attach a 2 × 4 piece of wood behind the top of the standpipe for support, using 2½" deck screws. Fasten standpipe to the wood support, using a length of pipe strap and ½" screws. Insert the washing machine's rubber drain hose into the standpipe.

How to Make Water Supply Connections

Install hose bibs in the utility sink supply lines. Turn off water main and drain pipes. Cut into each supply pipe 6" to 12" from faucet. Solder threaded T-fittings into each supply line (pages 46 to 50). Protect wood from torch flame with two layers of sheet metal. Wrap Teflon tape around threads of hose bibs, and screw them into T-fittings. Connect a rubber supply hose from each bib to appropriate intake valve on washing machine.

Recessed-mounted washing machine boxes are available for finished utility rooms. The supply pipes and standpipe drain run to one central location. The washing machine's hose bibs, supply hoses, and drain hose must remain easily accessible.

Vacuum breaker

Valve box

¾" flexible PE pipe

Drain-and-waste control valve

Installing Outdoor Plumbing

Flexible polyethylene (PE) pipe (pages 62 to 63) is used to extend cold water plumbing lines to an outdoor fixture, such as a sink located in a shed or detached garage, a lawn sprinkler system, or a garden spigot. In mild climates, outdoor plumbing can remain in service year-round, but in regions with a frost season, the outdoor supply pipes must be drained or blown empty with pressurized air to prevent the pipes from rupturing when the ground freezes in winter.

On the following pages you will see how to run supply pipes from the house to a utility sink in a detached garage. The utility sink drains into a rock-filled *dry well* installed in the yard. A dry well is designed to handle only "gray water" waste, such as the soapy rinse water created by washing tools or work clothes. Never use a dry

well drain for septic materials, such as animal waste or food scraps. Never pour paints, solvent-based liquids, or solid materials into a sink that drains into a dry well. Such materials will quickly clog up your system and will eventually filter down into the groundwater supply.

Like an indoor sink, the garage utility sink has a vent pipe running up from the drain trap. This vent can extend through the roof (page 197), or it can extend through the side wall of the garage and be covered with a screen to keep birds and insects out.

Before digging a trench for an outdoor plumbing line, contact your local utility companies and ask them to mark the locations of underground gas, power, telephone, and water lines.

174

Vent pipe

Valve box

Drain trap

Waste T-fitting

Landscape fabric

PVC drain pipe

Dry well filled with coarse rock

Underground lawn sprinkler systems can be installed using the same basic techniques used for plumbing an outdoor utility sink. Sprinkler systems vary from manufacturer to manufacturer, so make sure to follow the product recommendations when planning your system. See page 179.

How to Install Outdoor Plumbing for a Garage Sink

1 Plan a convenient route from a basement ¾"- cold-water supply pipe to the outdoor sink location, then drill a 1"-diameter hole through the sill plate. Drill a similar hole where the pipe will enter the garage. On the ground outside, lay out the pipe run with spray paint or stakes.

2 Use a flat spade to remove sod for an 8"- to 12"-wide trench along the marked route from the house to the garage. Set the sod aside and keep it moist so it can be reused after the project is completed. Dig a trench that slopes slightly (⅛" per ft.) toward the house and is at least 10" deep at its shallowest point. Use a long, straight 2 × 4 and level to ensure that the trench has the correct slope.

3 Below the access hole in the rim joist, dig a small pit and install a plastic valve box so the top is flush with the ground. Lay a thick layer of gravel in the bottom of the box. Dig a similar pit and install a second valve box at the opposite end of the trench, where the water line will enter the garage.

4 Run ¾" PE pipe along the bottom of the trench from the house to the utility sink location. Use insert couplings and stainless steel clamps when it is necessary to join two lengths of pipe.

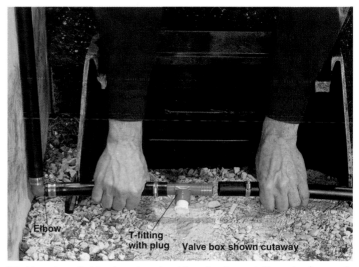

Elbow

T-fitting with plug   **Valve box shown cutaway**

TIP: To run pipe under a sidewalk, attach a length of rigid PVC pipe to a garden hose with a pipe-to-hose adapter. Cap the end of the pipe, and drill a ⅛" hole in the center of the cap. Turn on the water, and use the high-pressure stream to bore a tunnel.

5 At each end of the trench, extend the pipe through the valve box and up the foundation wall, using a barbed elbow fitting to make the 90° bend. Install a barbed T-fitting with a threaded outlet in the valve box, so the threaded portion of the fitting faces down. Insert a male threaded plug in the bottom outlet of the T-fitting. See pages 62 to 63 for directions on joining PE pipe and fittings.

Vacuum breaker

Female threaded adapter (copper)

Drain-and-waste valve

Male threaded adapter (PVC)

6 Use barbed elbow fittings to extend the pipe into the basement and garage, then use pipe straps and masonry screws to anchor the PE pipe to the foundation.

7 Inside the house, make the transition between the PE pipe and the copper cold water supply pipe, using a threaded male PVC adapter, a female threaded copper adapter, a vacuum breaker, a drain-and-waste valve, and a copper T-fitting, as shown. The drain-and-waste valve includes a threaded cap, which can be removed to blow water from the lines when you winterize the system.

(continued next page)

How to Install Outdoor Plumbing for a Garage Sink (continued)

8 In the garage, attach a male threaded PVC adapter to the end of the PE pipe, then use a copper female threaded adapter, elbow, and male threaded adapter to extend a copper riser up to a brass hose bib. After completing the supply pipe installation, fill in the trench, tamping the soil firmly. Install the utility sink, complete with 1½" drain trap and waste T-fitting (page 175). Bore a 2" hole in the wall where the sink drain will exit the garage.

9 At least 6 ft. from the garage, dig a pit about 2 ft. in diameter and 3 ft. deep. Punch holes in the sides and bottom of an old trash can, and cut a 2" hole in the side of the can, about 4" from the top edge. Insert the can into the pit; the top edge should be about 6" below ground level. Run 1½" PVC drain pipe from the utility sink to the dry well (page 175). Fill the dry well with coarse rock, drape landscape fabric over it, then cover the trench and well with soil and reinstall the sod. Extend a vent pipe up from the waste T through the roof or side wall of the garage (page 197).

How to Winterize Outdoor Plumbing Pipes in Cold Climates

Close the drain-and-waste valve for the outdoor supply pipe, then remove the cap on the drain nipple. With the hose bib on the outdoor sink open, attach an air compressor to the valve nipple, then blow water from the system using no more than 50 psi (pounds per square inch) of air pressure. Remove the plugs from the T-fittings in each valve box, and store them for the winter.

Components of an Underground Sprinkler System

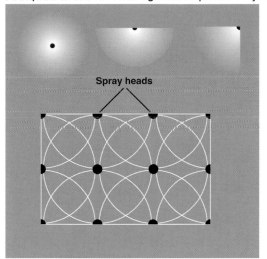

System layout is crucial to ensure proper irrigation of all parts of your yard. Spray heads are available in full-circle, semi-circle, or quarter-circle patterns to cover the entire space. In most cases, you will divide your landscape into several individual zones, each controlled by its own valve. With a timer (photo below), you can program precise start and stop times for each irrigation zone.

Valve manifold is a group of valves used to control the various sprinkler zones. Some models are installed below ground in a valve box, while others extend above the ground. When a timer is used, each control valve in the manifold is wired separately into the timer.

Sprinkler timers can be programmed to provide automatic control of all zones in an underground sprinkler system. Deluxe models control up to 16 different zones and have rain sensors that shut off the system when irrigation is not needed.

Sprinkler heads come in many styles to provide a variety of spray patterns. Flexible underground tubing, sometimes called *funny pipe*, links the spray head to saddle fittings on the underground water supply pipes.

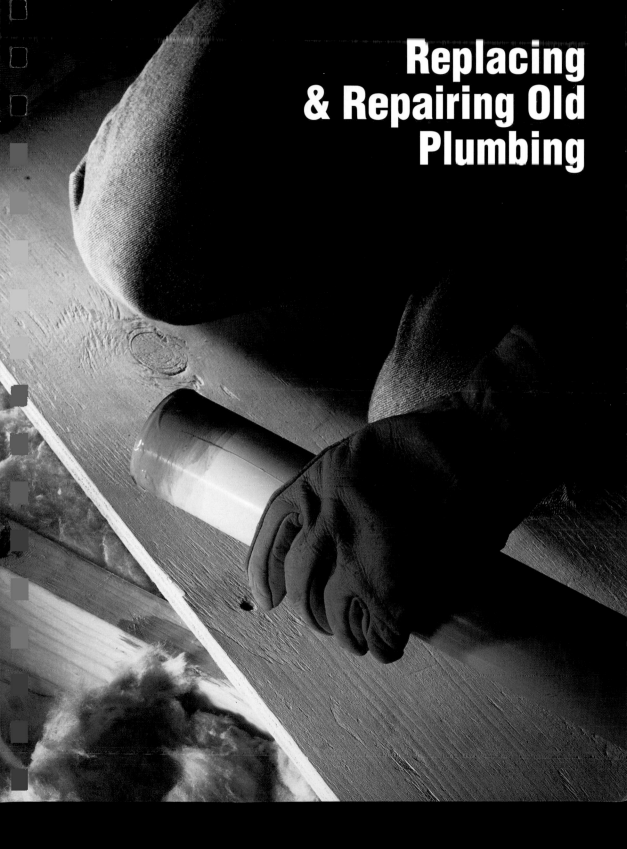

Replacing
& Repairing Old
Plumbing

Replacing Old Plumbing

Plumbing pipes, like all building materials, eventually wear out and have to be replaced. If you find yourself repairing leaky, corroded pipes every few months, it may be time to consider replacing the old system entirely—and soon. A corroded water pipe that bursts while you are away can cost you many thousands of dollars in damage to wall surfaces, framing members, and furnishings.

Identifying the materials used in your plumbing system can also tell you if replacement is advised. If you have galvanized steel pipes, for example, it is a good bet that they will need to be replaced in the near future. Most galvanized steel pipes were installed before 1960, and since steel pipes have a maximum life expectancy of 30 to 35 years, such a system is probably living on borrowed time. On the other hand, if your system includes copper supply pipes and plastic drain pipes, you can relax; these materials were likely installed within the last 30 years, and they are considerably more durable than steel, provided they were installed correctly.

Replacing old plumbing nearly always involves some demolition and carpentry work. Even in the best scenario, you probably will find it necessary to open walls and floors in order to run new pipes. For this reason, replacing old plumbing is often done at the same time as a kitchen or bathroom remodeling project, when wall and floor surfaces have to be removed and replaced. If possible, leave old plumbing pipes in place. To save time, professional plumbing contractors remove old pipes only when they interfere with the routing of the new plumbing lines.

A plumbing renovation project is subject to the same code regulations as a new installation. Always work in conjunction with your local inspector (pages 24 to 29) when replacing old plumbing.

This section shows:

Replacement Options

Partial replacement involves replacing only those sections of your plumbing system that are currently causing problems. This is a quick, less-expensive option than a complete renovation, but it is only a temporary solution. Old plumbing will continue to fail until you replace the entire system.

Complete replacement of all plumbing lines is an ambitious job, but doing this work yourself can save you thousands of dollars. To minimize the inconvenience, you can do this work in phases, replacing one branch of the plumbing system at a time.

Evaluating Your Plumbing

Fixture Units	Minimum Gallons per Minute (GPM)
10	8
15	11
20	14
25	17
30	20

By the time you spot the telltale evidence of a leaky drain pipe or water supply pipe, the damage to the walls and ceilings of your home can be considerable. The tips on the following pages show early warning signals that indicate your plumbing system is beginning to fail.

Proper evaluation of your plumbing helps you identify old, suspect materials and anticipate problems. It also can save you money and frustration. Replacing an old plumbing system at your convenience—before it reaches the disaster stage—is preferable to hiring a plumbing contractor to bail you out of an emergency situation.

Remember that the network of pipes running through the walls of your home is only one part of the larger system. You should also evaluate the main water supply and sewer pipes that connect your home to the city utility system and make sure they are adequate before you replace your plumbing.

Minimum recommended water capacity is based on total demand on the system, as measured by fixture units, a standard of measurement assigned by the plumbing code. First, add up the total units of all the fixtures in your plumbing system (page 26). Then, perform the water supply capacity test described below. Finally, compare your water capacity with the recommended minimums listed above. If the capacity falls below that recommended in the table above, then the main water supply pipe running from the city water main to your home is inadequate and should be replaced with a larger pipe by a licensed contractor.

How to Determine Your Water Supply Capacity

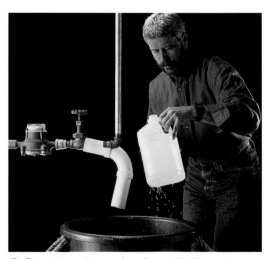

1 Shut off the water at the valve on your water meter, then disconnect the pipe on the house side of the meter. Construct a test spout using a 2" PVC elbow and two 6" lengths of 2" PVC pipe, then place the spout on the exposed outlet on the water meter. Place a large watertight tub under the spout to collect water.

2 Open the main supply valve and let the water run into the container for 30 seconds. Shut off the water, then measure the amount of water in the container and multiply this figure by 2. This number represents the gallons-per-minute (gpm) rate of your main water supply. Compare this measurement with the recommended capacity in the table above.

Rust stains on the surfaces of toilet bowls and sinks may indicate severe corrosion inside iron supply pipes. This symptom generally means your water supply system is likely to fail in the near future. NOTE: Rust stains can also be caused by a water heater problem or by a water supply with a high mineral content. Check for these problems before assuming your pipes are bad.

Low water pressure at fixtures suggests that the supply pipes either are badly clogged with rust and mineral deposits or are undersized. To measure water pressure, plug the fixture drain and open the faucets for 30 seconds. Measure the amount of water and multiply by 2; this figure is the gallons-per-minute rating. Vanity faucets should supply 1¾ gpm; bathtub faucets, 6 gpm; kitchen sink faucets, 4½ gpm.

Slow drains throughout the house may indicate that DWV pipes are badly clogged with rust and mineral deposits. When a fixture faucet is opened fully with the drains unstopped, water should not collect in tubs and basins. NOTE: Slow drains may also be the result of inadequate venting. Check for this problem before assuming the drain pipes are bad.

Backed-up floor drains indicate that the main sewer service to the street is clogged. If you have this problem regularly, have the main sewer lines evaluated by a plumbing contractor before you replace your house plumbing. The contractor will be able to determine if your sewer problem is a temporary clog or a more serious problem that requires major work.

Replacing Old Plumbing: A Step-by-step Overview

The overview sequence shown here represents the basic steps you will need to follow when replacing DWV and water supply pipes. On the following pages, you will see these steps demonstrated in complete detail, as we replace all the water supply pipes and drain pipes for a bathroom, including the main waste-vent stack running from basement to roofline.

Remember that no two plumbing jobs are ever alike, and your own project will probably differ from the demonstration projects shown in this section. Always work in conjunction with your local plumbing inspector, and organize your work around a detailed plumbing plan that shows the particulars of your project. Review pages 18 to 31 of this book before starting work.

How to Replace Old Plumbing: An Overview

1 Plan the routes for the new plumbing pipes. Creating efficient pathways for new pipes is crucial to a smooth installation. In some cases this requires removing wall or floor surfaces. Or, you can frame a false wall, called a *chase* (page 188), to create space for running the new pipes.

2 Remove sections of the old waste-vent stack, as needed, then install a new main waste-vent stack running from the main drain in the basement to the roof. Include the fittings necessary to connect branch drains and vent lines to the stack.

3 Install new branch drains from the waste-vent stack to the stub-outs for the individual fixtures. If the fixture locations have not changed, you may need to remove sections of the old drain pipes in order to run the new pipes.

4 Remove the old closet bend and replace it with a new bend running to the new waste vent stack. This task usually requires that you remove areas of flooring. Framing work may also be required to create a path for the toilet drain.

5 Replace the vent pipes running from the fixtures up to the attic, then connect them to the new waste-vent stack.

6 Install new copper supply lines running from the water meter to all fixture locations. Test the DWV and water supply pipes and have your work inspected before closing up walls and installing the fixtures.

Planning Pipe Routes

Build a framed chase. A chase is a false wall created to provide space for new plumbing pipes. It is especially effective for installing a new main waste-vent stack. On a two-story house, chases can be stacked one over the other on each floor in order to run plumbing from the basement to the attic. Once plumbing is completed and inspected, the chase is covered with wallboard and finished to match the room.

The first, and perhaps most important, step when replacing old plumbing is to decide how and where to run the new pipes. Since the stud cavities and joist spaces are often covered with finished wall surfaces, finding routes for running new pipes can be challenging.

When planning pipe routes, choose straight, easy pathways whenever possible. Rather than running water supply pipes around wall corners and through studs, for example, it may be easiest to run them straight up wall cavities from the basement. Instead of running a bathtub drain across floor joists, run it straight down into the basement, where the branch drain can be easily extended underneath the joists to the main waste-vent stack.

In some situations, it is most practical to route the new pipes in wall and floor cavities that already hold plumbing pipes, since these spaces often are framed to provide long, unobstructed runs. A detailed map of your plumbing system can be very helpful when planning routes for new plumbing pipes (pages 18 to 23).

To maximize their profits, plumbing contractors generally try to avoid opening walls or changing wall framing when installing new plumbing. But the do-it-yourselfer does not have these limitations. Faced with the difficulty of running pipes through enclosed spaces, you may find it easiest to remove wall surfaces or to create a newly framed space for running new pipes.

On these pages, you will see some common methods used to create pathways for replacing old pipes with new plumbing.

Use existing access panels to disconnect fixtures and remove old pipes. Plan the location of new fixtures and pipe runs to make use of existing access panels, minimizing the amount of demolition and repair work you will need to do.

Convert a laundry chute into a channel for running new plumbing pipes. The door of the chute can be used to provide access to control valves, or it can be removed and covered with wall materials, then finished to match the surrounding wall.

Run pipes inside a closet. If they are unobtrusive, pipes can be left exposed at the back of the closet. Or, you can frame a chase to hide the pipes after the installation is completed.

Remove suspended ceiling panels to route new plumbing pipes in joist cavities. Or, you can route pipes across a standard plaster or wallboard ceiling, then construct a false ceiling to cover the installation, provided there is adequate height. Most building codes require a minimum of 7 ft. from floor to finished ceiling.

(continued next page)

Tips for Planning Pipe Routes (continued)

Use a drill extension and spade bit or hole saw to drill through wall plates from unfinished attic or basement spaces above or below the wall.

Look for "wet walls." Walls that hold old plumbing pipes can be good choices for running long vertical runs of new pipe. These spaces usually are open, without obstacles such as fireblocks and insulation.

Probe wall and floor cavities with a long piece of plastic pipe to ensure that a clear pathway exists for running new pipe (left). Once you have established a route using the narrow pipe, you can use the pipe as a guide when running larger drain pipes up into the wall (right).

Remove flooring when necessary. Because replacing toilet and bathtub drains usually requires that you remove sections of floor, a full plumbing replacement job is often done in conjunction with a complete bathroom remodeling project.

Remove wall surfaces when access from above or below the wall is not possible. This demolition work can range from cutting narrow channels in plaster or wallboard to removing the entire wall surface. Remove wall surfaces back to the centers of adjoining studs; the exposed studs provide a nailing surface for attaching repair materials once the plumbing project is completed.

Create a detailed map showing the planned route for your new plumbing pipes. Such a map can help you get your plans approved by the inspector, and it makes work much simpler. If you have already mapped your existing plumbing system (pages 18 to 23), those drawings can be used to plan new pipe routes.

Replacing a Main Waste-vent Stack

Although a main waste-vent stack rarely rusts through entirely, it can be nearly impossible to join new branch drains and vents to an old cast iron stack. For this reason, plumbing contractors sometimes recommend replacing the iron stack with plastic pipe during a plumbing renovation project.

Be aware that replacing a main waste-vent stack is not an easy job (pages 75 to 77). You will be cutting away heavy sections of cast iron, so working with a helper is essential. Before beginning work, make sure you have a complete plan for your plumbing system and have designed a stack that includes all the fittings you will need to connect branch drains and vent pipes. While work is in progress, none of your plumbing fixtures will be usable. To speed up the project and minimize inconvenience, do as much of the demolition and preliminary construction work as you can before starting work on the stack.

Because main waste-vent stacks may be as large as 4" in diameter, running a new stack through existing walls can be troublesome. To solve this problem, our project employs a common solution: framing a chase in the corner of a room to provide the necessary space for running the new stack from the basement to the attic. When the installation is completed, the chase will be finished with wallboard to match the room.

A new main waste-vent stack is best installed near the location of the old stack. In this way, the new stack can be connected to the basement floor cleanout fitting used by the old cast iron stack.

1 Secure the cast iron waste-vent stack near the ceiling of your basement, using a riser clamp installed between the floor joists (page 75). Use wood blocks attached to the joists with 3" wallboard screws to support the clamp. Also clamp the stack in the attic, at the point where the stack passes down into the wall cavity. WARNING: A cast iron stack running from basement to attic can weigh several hundred pounds. Never cut into a cast iron stack before securing it with riser clamps above the cut.

2 Use a cast iron snap cutter (page 76) or a reciprocating saw to sever the stack near the floor of the basement, about 8" above the cleanout, and near the ceiling, flush with the bottom of the joists. Have a helper hold the stack while you are cutting out the section. NOTE: After cutting into the main stack, plug the open end of the pipe with a cloth to prevent sewer gases from rising into your home.

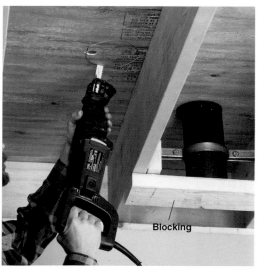

Blocking

3 Nail blocking against the bottom of the joists across the severed stack. Then, cut a 6"-diameter hole in the basement ceiling where the new waste-vent stack will run, using a reciprocating saw. Suspend a plumb bob at the centerpoint of the opening as a guide for aligning the new stack.

(continued next page)

193

4 Attach a 5-ft. segment of PVC plastic pipe the same diameter as the old waste-vent stack to the exposed end of the cast iron cleanout fitting, using a banded coupling with neoprene sleeve (page 76).

5 Dry-fit 45° elbows and straight lengths of plastic pipe to offset the new stack, lining it up with the plumb bob centered on the ceiling opening.

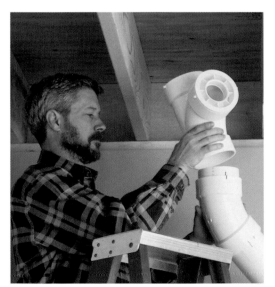

6 Dry-fit a waste T-fitting on the stack, with the inlets necessary for any branch drains that will be connected in the basement. Make sure the fitting is positioned at a height that will allow the branch drains to have the correct ¼" per ft. downward slope toward the stack.

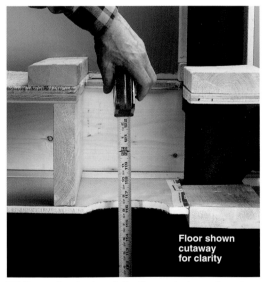

Floor shown cutaway for clarity

7 Determine the length for the next piece of waste-vent pipe by measuring from the basement T-fitting to the next planned fitting in the vertical run. In our project, we installed a T-fitting between floor joists, where the toilet drain was connected.

8 Cut a PVC plastic pipe to length, raise it into the opening, and dry-fit it to the T fitting. NOTE: For very long pipe runs, you may need to construct this vertical run by solvent-gluing two or more segments of pipe together with couplings.

9 Check the length of the stack, then solvent-glue all fittings together. Support the new stack with a riser clamp resting on blocks attached between basement ceiling joists.

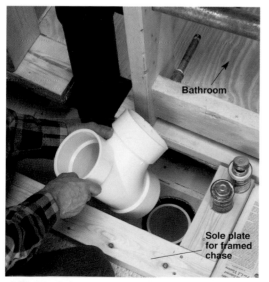

Bathroom

Sole plate for framed chase

10 Attach the next waste T-fitting to the stack. In our demonstration project, the waste T lay between floor joists and was used to connect the toilet drain. Make sure the waste T is positioned at a height that will allow for the correct ¼" per ft. downward slope for the toilet drain.

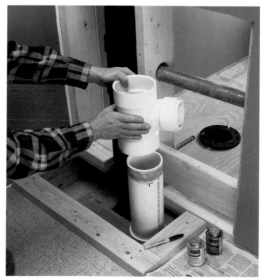

11 Add additional lengths of pipe, with waste T-fittings installed where other fixtures will drain into the stack. In our example, a waste T with a 1½" bushing insert was installed where the vanity sink drain was attached to the stack. Make sure the T-fittings are positioned to allow for the correct downward pitch of the branch drains.

(continued next page)

12 Cut a hole in the ceiling where the waste-vent stack will extend into the attic, then measure, cut, and solvent-glue the next length of pipe in place. The pipe should extend at least 1 ft. up into the attic.

13 Remove the roof flashing from around the old waste-vent stack. You may need to remove shingles in order to accomplish this. NOTE: Always use caution when working on a roof. If you are unsure of your ability to do this work, hire a roof repair specialist to remove the old flashing and install new flashing around the new vent pipe.

14 In the attic, remove old vent pipes, where necessary, then sever the cast iron soil stack with a cast iron cutter, and lower the stack down from the roof opening with the aid of a helper. Support the old stack with a riser clamp installed between joists.

15 Solvent-glue a vent T with a 1½" bushing in the side inlet to the top of the new waste-vent stack. The side inlet should point toward the nearest auxiliary vent pipe extending up from below.

16 Finish the waste-vent stack installation by using 45° elbows and straight lengths of pipe to extend the stack through the same roof opening used by the old vent stack. The new stack should extend at least 1 ft. through the roof, but no more than 2 ft.

How to Flash a Waste-vent Stack

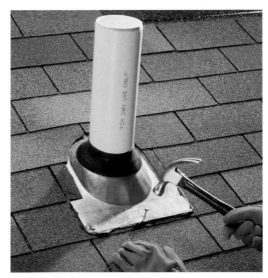

1 Loosen the shingles directly above the new vent stack, and remove any nails, using a flat pry bar. When installed, the metal vent flashing will lie flat on the shingles surrounding the vent pipe. Apply roofing cement to the underside of the flashing.

2 Slide the flashing over the vent pipe, and carefully tuck the base of the flashing up under the shingles. Press the flange firmly against the roof deck to spread the roofing cement, then anchor it with rubber gasket flashing nails. Reattach loose shingles as necessary.

Replacing Branch Drains & Vent Pipes

In our demonstration project, we will replace branch drains for a bathtub and vanity sink. The tub drain will run down into the basement before connecting to the main waste-vent stack, while the vanity drain will run horizontally to connect directly to the stack.

A vent pipe for the bathtub runs up into the attic, where it will join the main waste-vent stack. The vanity sink, however, requires no secondary vent pipe, since its location falls within the critical distance (page 29) of the new waste-vent stack.

Remove old pipes only where they obstruct the planned route for the new pipes. You will probably have to remove drain and water supply pipes at each fixture location, but the remaining pipes usually can be left in place. A reciprocating saw with metal-cutting blade works well for this job.

How to Replace Branch Drains

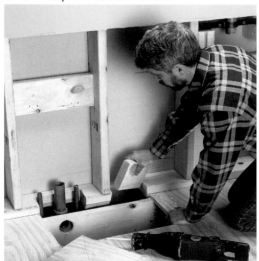

1 Establish a route for vertical drain pipes running through wall cavities down into the basement. For our project, we cut away a section of the wall sole plate in order to run a 1½" bathtub drain pipe from the basement up to the bathroom.

2 From the basement, cut a hole in the bottom of the wall, below the opening cut (step 1). Measure, cut, and insert a length of vertical drain pipe up into the wall to the bathroom. A length of flexible CPVC pipe can be useful for guiding the drain pipe up into the wall. For very long pipe runs, you may need to join two or more lengths of pipe with couplings as you insert the run.

3 Secure the vertical drain pipe with a riser clamp supported on 2 × 4 blocks nailed between joists (page 75). Take care not to overtighten the clamps.

4 Install a horizontal pipe from the waste T-fitting on the waste-vent stack to the vertical drain pipe. Maintain a downward slope toward the stack of ¼" per ft., and use a Y-fitting with 45° elbow to form a cleanout where the horizontal and vertical drain pipes meet.

5 Solvent-glue a waste T-fitting to the top of the vertical drain pipe. For a bathtub drain, as shown here, the T-fitting must be well below floor level to allow for the bathtub drain trap (page 114). You may need to notch or cut a hole in floor joists to connect the drain trap to the waste T (page 82).

6 From the attic, cut a hole into the top of the bathroom wet wall, directly above the bathtub drain pipe. Run a 1½" vent pipe down to the bathtub location, and solvent-glue it to the waste T. Make sure the pipe extends at least 1 ft. into the attic.

(continued next page)

How to Replace Branch Drains (continued)

7 Remove wall surfaces as necessary to provide access for running horizontal drain pipes from fixtures to the new waste-vent stack. In our project, we ran 1½" drain pipe from a vanity sink to the stack.

Mark the drain route on the exposed studs, maintaining a ¼" per ft. downward slope toward the stack. Use a reciprocating saw or jig saw to notch out the studs (page 82).

8 Secure the old drain and vent pipes with riser clamps supported by blocking attached between the studs.

9 Remove the old drain and water supply pipes, where necessary, to provide space for running the new drain pipes.

10 Using a sweep elbow and straight length of pipe, assemble a drain pipe to run from the drain stub-out location to the waste T-fitting on the new waste-vent stack. Use a 90° elbow and a short length of pipe to create a stub-out extending at least 2" out from the wall. Secure the stub-out to a ¾" backer board attached between studs.

11 Protect the drain pipes by attaching metal protector plates over the notches in the studs. Protector plates prevent drain pipes from being punctured when wall surfaces are replaced.

12 In the attic, use a vent elbow and straight length of pipe to connect the vertical vent pipe from the tub to the new waste-vent stack.

Replacing a Toilet Drain

Replacing a toilet drain is sometimes a troublesome task, mostly because the cramped space makes it difficult to route the large, 3" or 4" pipe. You likely will need to remove flooring around the toilet and wall surface behind the toilet.

Replacing a toilet drain may require framing work, as well, if you find it necessary to cut into joists in order to route the new pipes. When possible, plan your project to avoid changes to the framing members.

Replacing a toilet drain usually requires that you remove flooring and wall surface to gain access to the pipes.

How to Replace a Toilet Drain

1 Remove the toilet, then unscrew the toilet flange from the floor and remove it from the drain pipe. NOTE: If the existing toilet flange is cast iron or bronze, it may be joined to the closet bend with poured lead or solder; in this case, it is easiest to break up the flange with a masonry hammer (make sure to wear eye protection) and remove it in pieces.

Joist location

2 Cut away the flooring around the toilet drain along the center of the floor joists, using a circular saw with the blade set to a depth ⅛" more than the thickness of the subfloor. The exposed joist will serve as a nailing surface when the subfloor is replaced.

3 Cut away the old closet bend as close as possible to the old waste-vent stack, using a reciprocating saw with metal-cutting blade, or a cast iron cutter.

4 If a joist obstructs the route to the new waste-vent stack, cut away a section of the floor joist. Install double headers and metal joist hangers to support the ends of the cut joist.

5 Create a new toilet drain running to the new waste-vent stack, using a closet bend and a straight length of pipe. Position the drain so there will be at least 15" of space between the center of the bowl and side wall surfaces when the toilet is installed. Make sure the drain slopes at least ¼" per ft. toward the stack, then support the pipe with plastic pipe strap attached to framing members. Insert a 6" length of pipe in the top inlet of the closet bend; once the new drain pipes have been tested, this pipe will be cut off with a handsaw and fitted with a toilet flange.

6 Cut a piece of exterior-grade plywood to fit the cutout floor area, and use a jig saw to cut an opening for the toilet drain stubout. Position the plywood, and attach it to joists and blocking with 2" screws.

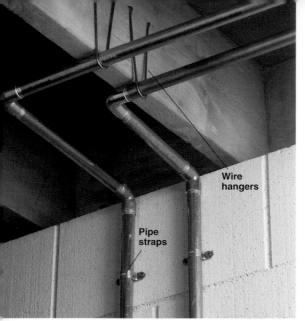

Support copper supply pipes at least every 10 ft. along vertical runs and 6 ft. along horizontal runs (check local codes). Always use copper or plastic support materials with copper; never use steel, which can interact with copper and cause corrosion.

Replacing Supply Pipes

When replacing old galvanized water supply pipes, we recommend that you use Type M rigid copper or PEX (see pages 64 to 69). Use ¾" pipe for the main distribution pipes and ½" pipes for the branch lines running to individual fixtures.

For convenience, run hot and cold water pipes parallel to one another, between 3" and 6" apart. Use the straightest, most direct routes possible when planning the layout, because too many bends in the pipe runs can cause significant friction and reduce water pressure.

It is a good idea to remove old supply pipes that are exposed, but pipes hidden in walls can be left in place unless they interfere with the installation of the new supply pipes.

How to Replace Water Supply Pipes

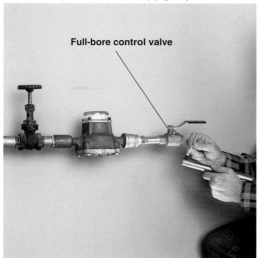

1 Shut off the water on the street side of the water meter, then disconnect and remove the old water pipes from the house side. Solder a ¾" male threaded adapter and full-bore control valve to a short length of ¾" copper pipe, then attach this assembly to the house side of the water meter. Extend the ¾" cold-water distribution pipe toward the nearest fixture, which is usually the water heater.

2 At the water heater, install a ¾" T-fitting in the cold-water distribution pipe. Use two lengths of ¾" copper pipe and a full-bore control valve to run a branch pipe to the water heater. From the outlet opening on the water heater, extend a ¾" hot water distribution pipe, also with a full-bore control valve (page 40). Continue the hot and cold supply lines on parallel routes toward the next group of fixtures in your house.

3 Establish routes for branch supply lines by drilling holes into stud cavities. Install T-fittings, then begin the branch lines by installing brass control valves. Branch lines should be made with ¾" pipe if they are supplying more than one fixture; ½" if they are supplying only one fixture.

4 Extend the branch lines to the fixtures. In our project, we ran ¾" vertical branch lines up through the framed chase to the bathroom. Route pipes around obstacles, such as a main waste-vent stack, by using 45° and 90° elbows and short lengths of pipe.

5 Where branch lines run through studs or floor joists, drill holes or cut notches in the framing members (page 82), then insert the pipes. For long runs of pipe, you may need to join two or more shorter lengths of pipe, using couplings as you create the runs.

6 Install ¾" to ½" reducing T-fittings and elbows to extend the branch lines to individual fixtures. In our bathroom, we installed a hot and cold stub-out for the bathtub and sink, and a cold-water stub-out for the toilet. Cap each stub-out until your work has been inspected and the wall surfaces have been completed.

Repairing Existing Plumbing

Every homeowner eventually deals with plumbing problems. Most can be repaired with basic skills, tools, and instructions and require no professional help. This section will help you recognize and fix problems with all types of common household plumbing fixtures.

On the following pages you'll find directions for repairing faucets, including shutoff valves, supply tubes, diverter valves, sprayers, and aerators. The information on tub and shower plumbing includes directions for repairing tub and shower faucets, plus showerheads. For problems with an outdoor water supply, see the directions for repairing valves, hose bibs, and sillcocks.

Toilet problems, too, are easily remedied. We'll show you how to adjust and replace toilet parts and how to stop a toilet from running or leaking.

The section on clogs includes detailed instructions for clearing all types of drains and for fixing separate drain system parts.

Because water heaters are usually out of sight, they are easy to ignore—until something goes wrong. This section shows how water heaters work, and how to repair or replace them. The section ends with advice on fixing burst, frozen, or noisy plumbing pipes.

Faucet Problems & Repairs

Most faucet problems are easy to fix. You can save money and time by making these simple repairs yourself. Replacement parts for faucet repairs usually are inexpensive and readily available at hardware stores and home centers. Techniques for repair vary, depending on the faucet design (page 209).

If a badly worn faucet continues to leak, even after repairs are made, the faucet should be replaced. In less than an hour, you can replace an old, problem faucet with a new model that is designed to provide years of trouble-free service.

Problems	Repairs
Faucet drips from the end of the spout or leaks around the base.	Identify the faucet design (page 209), then install replacement parts, using directions on the following pages.
Old worn-out faucet continues to leak after repairs are made.	Replace the old faucet (pages 220 to 223).
Water pressure at spout seems low, or water flow is partially blocked.	1. Clean faucet aerator (page 226). 2. Replace corroded galvanized pipes with copper (pages 46 to 51).
Water pressure from sprayer seems low, or sprayer leaks from handle.	1. Clean sprayer head (page 226). 2. Fix diverter valve (page 227).
Water leaks onto floor underneath faucet.	1. Replace cracked sprayer hose (page 227). 2. Tighten water connections, or replace supply tubes and shutoff valves (pages 224 to 225). 3. Fix leaky sink strainer (page 257).
Hose bib or valve drips from spout or leaks around handle.	Take valve apart and replace washers and O-rings (pages 238 to 239).

Fixing Leaky Faucets

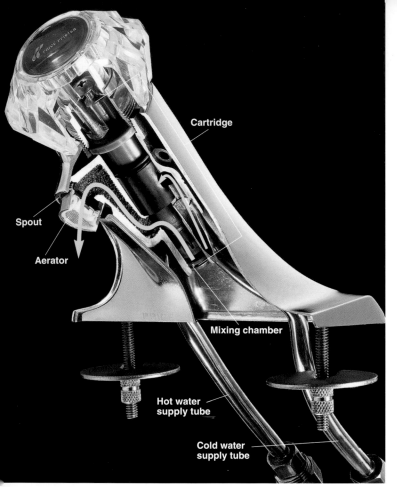

A leaky faucet is the most common home plumbing problem. Leaks occur when washers, O-rings, or seals inside the faucet are dirty or worn. Fixing leaks is easy, but the techniques for making repairs will vary, depending on the design of the faucet. Before beginning work, you must first identify your faucet design and determine what replacement parts are needed.

Typical faucet has a single handle attached to a hollow cartridge. The cartridge controls hot and cold water flowing from the supply tubes into the mixing chamber. Water is forced out the spout and through the aerator. When repairs are needed, replace the entire cartridge.

There are four basic faucet designs: ball-type, cartridge, disc, and compression. Many faucets can be identified easily by outer appearance, but others must be taken apart before the design can be recognized.

The compression design is used in many double-handle faucets. Compression faucets all have washers or seals that must be replaced from time to time. These repairs are easy to make, and replacement parts are inexpensive.

Ball-type, cartridge, and disc faucets are all known as washerless faucets. Many washerless faucets are controlled with a single handle, although some cartridge models use two handles. Washerless faucets are more trouble-free than compression faucets and are designed for quick repair.

Turn off water before starting any faucet repair, using shutoff valves underneath faucet, or main service valve found near water meter (page 12). When opening shutoff valves after finishing repairs, keep faucet handle in open position to release trapped air. When water runs steadily, close faucet.

When installing new faucet parts, make sure the replacements match the original parts. Replacement parts for popular washerless faucets are identified by brand name and model number. To ensure a correct selection, you may want to bring the worn parts to the store for comparison.

Specialty tools and materials for faucet repairs include penetrating oil (A), seat wrench (B), seat-dressing (reamer) tool (C), handle puller (D), plumber's putty (E), basin wrench (F), silicone caulk (G).

How to Identify Faucet Designs

Ball-type faucet has a single handle over a dome-shaped cap. If your single-handle faucet is made by Delta or Peerless, it is probably a ball-type faucet. See pages 210 to 211 to fix a ball-type faucet.

Cartridge faucets are available in single-handle or double-handle models. Popular cartridge faucet brands include Price Pfister, Moen, Valley, and Aqualine. See pages 212 to 213 to fix a cartridge faucet.

Compression faucet has two handles. When shutting the faucet off, you usually can feel a rubber washer being squeezed inside the faucet. Compression faucets are sold under many brand names. See pages 214 to 216 to fix a compression faucet.

Disc faucet has a single handle and a solid, chromed-brass body. If your faucet is made by American Standard or Reliant, it may be a disc faucet. See pages 218 to 219 to fix a disc faucet.

Setscrew

Knurled edges

Rounded cap

Spout

Cam

Cam washer

Ball

Valve seat

Valve seat

Spring

Spring

Spout O-rings

Ball-type faucet has a hollow ball that controls the temperature and flow of water. Dripping at the faucet spout is caused by worn-out valve seats, springs, or a damaged ball. Leaks around the base of the faucet are caused by worn O-rings.

Fixing Ball-type Faucets

A ball-type faucet has a single handle and is identified by the hollow metal or plastic ball inside the faucet body. Many ball-type faucets have a rounded cap with knurled edges located under the handle. If your faucet leaks from the spout and has this type of cap, first try tightening the cap with channel-type pliers. If tightening does not fix the leak, disassemble the faucet and install replacement parts.

Faucet manufacturers offer several types of replacement kits for ball-type faucets. Some kits contain only the springs and neoprene valve seats, while better kits also include the cam and cam washer.

Replace the rotating ball only if it is obviously worn or scratched. Replacement balls are either metal or plastic. Metal balls are slightly more expensive than plastic but are more durable.

Remember to turn off the water before beginning work (page 208).

Everything You Need

Tools: channel-type pliers, Allen wrench, screwdriver, utility knife.

Materials: ball-type faucet repair kit, new rotating ball (if needed), masking tape, O-rings, heatproof grease.

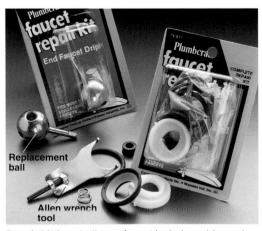

Replacement ball

Allen wrench tool

Repair kit for a ball-type faucet includes rubber valve seats, springs, cam, cam washer, and spout O-rings. Kit may also include small Allen wrench tool used to remove faucet handle. Make sure kit is made for your faucet model. Replacement ball can be purchased separately but is not needed unless old ball is obviously worn.

How to Fix a Ball-type Faucet

1 Loosen handle setscrew with an Allen wrench. Remove handle to expose faucet cap.

2 Remove the cap with channel-type pliers. To prevent scratches to the shiny chromed finish, wrap masking tape around the jaws of the pliers.

3 Lift out the faucet cam, cam washer, and the rotating ball. Check the ball for signs of wear.

4 Reach into the faucet with a screwdriver and remove the old springs and neoprene valve seats.

5 Remove spout by twisting it upward, then cut off old O-rings. Coat new O-rings with heatproof grease and install. Reattach spout, pressing downward until the collar rests on plastic slip ring. Install new springs and valve seats.

6 Insert ball, new cam washer, and cam. Small lug on cam should fit into notch on faucet body. Screw cap onto faucet and attach handle.

Index cap

Handle screw

Handle

Cartridge

Cartridge seal

Retaining ring

Spout

O-rings

Fixing Cartridge Faucets

A cartridge faucet is identified by the narrow metal or plastic cartridge inside the faucet body. Many single-handled faucets and some double-handle models use cartridge designs.

Replacing a cartridge is an easy repair that will fix most faucet leaks. Faucet cartridges come in many styles, so you may want to bring the old cartridge along for comparison when shopping for a replacement.

Make sure to insert the new cartridge so it is aligned in the same way as the old cartridge. If the hot and cold water controls are reversed, take the faucet apart and rotate the cartridge 180°.

Remember to turn off the water before beginning work (page 208).

Everything You Need

Tools: screwdriver, channel-type pliers, utility knife.

Materials: replacement cartridge, O-rings, heat-proof grease.

Cartridge faucet has a hollow cartridge insert that lifts and rotates to control the flow and temperature of water. Dripping at the spout occurs when the cartridge seals become worn. Leaks around the base of the faucet are caused by worn O-rings.

Replacement cartridges come in dozens of styles. Cartridges are available for popular faucet brands, including (from left) Price-Pfister, Moen, and Kohler. O-ring kits may be sold separately.

Handle screw

Index cap

1 Pry off the index cap on top of faucet, and remove the handle screw underneath the cap.

2 Remove faucet handle by lifting it up and tilting it backwards.

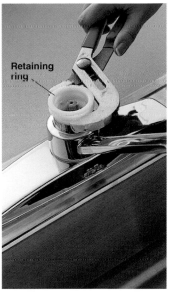

Retaining ring

3 Remove the threaded retaining ring with channel-type pliers. Remove any retaining clip holding cartridge in place.

Cartridge **Tab**

4 Grip top of the cartridge with channel-type pliers. Pull straight up to remove cartridge. Install replacement cartridge so that tab on cartridge faces forward.

O-rings

5 Remove the spout by pulling up and twisting, then cut off old O-rings with a utility knife. Coat new O-rings with heatproof grease, and install.

6 Reattach the spout. Screw the retaining ring onto the faucet, and tighten with channel-type pliers. Attach the handle, handle screw, and index cap.

213

Index cap

Handle screw

Handle

Retaining nut

Threaded spindle

Stem assembly

O-ring

Stem washer

Stem screw

Valve seat

A compression faucet has a stem assembly that includes a retaining nut, threaded spindle, O-ring, stem washer, and stem screw. Dripping at the spout occurs when the washer becomes worn. Leaks around the handle are caused by a worn O-ring.

Fixing Compression Faucets

Compression faucets have separate controls for hot and cold water and are identified by the threaded stem assemblies inside the faucet body. Compression stems come in many different styles, but all have some type of neoprene washer or seal to control water flow. Compression faucets leak when stem washers and seals become worn.

Older compression faucets often have corroded handles that are difficult to remove. A specialty tool called a handle puller makes this job easier. Handle pullers may be available at rental centers.

When replacing washers, also check the condition of the metal valve seats inside the faucet body. If the valve seats feel rough, they should be replaced or resurfaced.

Remember to turn off the water before beginning work (page 208).

Everything You Need

Tools: screwdriver, handle puller (if needed), channel-type pliers, utility knife, seat wrench or seat-dressing tool (if needed).

Materials: universal washer kit, packing string, heatproof grease, replacement valve seats (if needed).

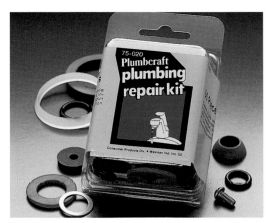

Universal washer kit contains parts needed to fix most types of compression faucets. Choose a kit that has an assortment of neoprene washers, O-rings, packing washers, and brass stem screws.

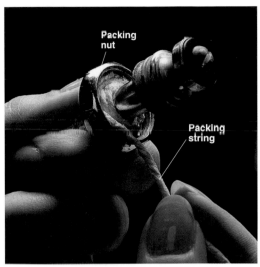

Remove stubborn handles with a handle puller. Remove the faucet index cap and handle screw, and clamp the side bars of the puller under the handle. Thread the puller into the faucet stem, and tighten until the handle comes free.

Packing string is used instead of an O-ring on some faucets. To fix leaks around the faucet handle, wrap new packing string around the stem, just underneath the packing nut or retaining nut.

Three Common Types of Compression Stems

Standard stem has a brass stem screw that holds either a flat or beveled neoprene washer to the end of the spindle. If stem screw is worn, it should be replaced.

Tophat stem has a snap-on neoprene diaphragm instead of a standard washer. Fix leaks by replacing the diaphragm.

Reverse-pressure stem has a beveled washer at the end of the spindle. To replace washer, unscrew spindle from rest of the stem assembly. Some stems have a small nut that holds washer.

215

How to Fix a Compression Faucet

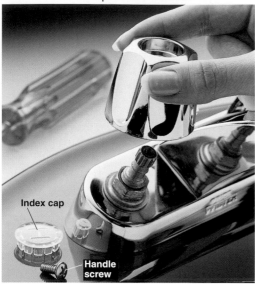

1 Remove index cap from top of faucet handle, and remove handle screw. Remove handle by pulling straight up. If necessary, use a handle puller to remove handle (page 215).

Index cap

Handle screw

2 Unscrew the stem assembly from body of faucet, using channel-type pliers. Inspect valve seat for wear, and replace or resurface as needed (page opposite). If faucet body or stems are badly worn, it usually is best to replace the faucet (pages 220 to 223).

Stem assembly

Brass stem screw

Stem washer

3 Remove the brass stem screw from the stem assembly. Remove worn stem washer.

Retaining nut

Threaded spindle

4 Unscrew the threaded spindle from the retaining nut.

O-ring

5 Cut off O-ring and replace with an exact duplicate. Install new washer and stem screw. Coat all parts with heatproof grease, then reassemble the faucet.

1 Check valve seat for damage by running a finger-tip around the rim of the seat. If the valve seat feels rough, replace the seat, or resurface it with a seat-dressing (reamer) tool (below).

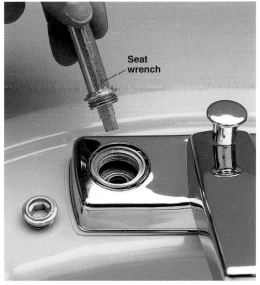

2 Remove valve seat, using a seat wrench. Select end of wrench that fits seat, and insert into faucet. Turn counterclockwise to remove seat, then install an exact duplicate. If seat cannot be removed, resurface with a seat-dressing tool (below).

How to Resurface Valve Seats

1 Select cutter head to fit the inside diameter of re-taining nut. Slide retaining nut over threaded shaft of seat-dressing tool, then attach the locknut and cut-ter head to the shaft.

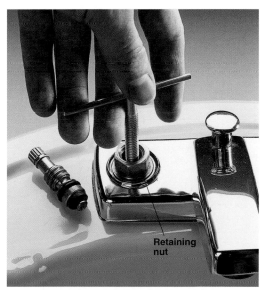

2 Screw retaining nut loosely into faucet body. Press the tool down lightly and turn tool handle clockwise two or three rotations. Reassemble faucet.

Fixing Disc Faucets

A disc faucet has a single handle and is identified by the wide cylinder inside the faucet body. The cylinder contains a pair of closely fitting ceramic discs that control the flow of water.

A ceramic disc faucet is a top-quality fixture that is easy to repair. Leaks usually can be fixed by lifting out the cylinder and cleaning the neoprene seals and the cylinder openings. Install a new cylinder only if the faucet continues to leak after cleaning.

After making repairs to a disc faucet, make sure handle is in the ON position, then open the shut-off valves slowly. Otherwise, ceramic discs can be cracked by the sudden release of air from the faucet. When water runs steadily, close the faucet.

Remember to turn off the water before beginning work (page 208).

Everything You Need

Tools: screwdriver.

Materials: fiber abrasive pad, replacement cylinder (if needed).

Disc faucet has a sealed cylinder containing two closely fitting ceramic discs. Faucet handle controls water by sliding the discs into alignment. Dripping at the spout occurs when the neoprene seals or cylinder openings are dirty.

Replacement cylinder for disc faucet is necessary only if faucet continues to leak after cleaning. Continuous leaking is caused by cracked or scratched ceramic discs. Replacement cylinders come with neoprene seals and mounting screws.

How to Fix a Ceramic Disc Faucet

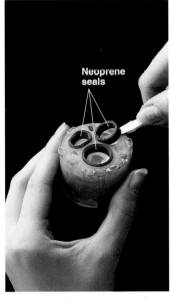

1 Rotate faucet spout to the side, and raise the handle. Remove the setscrew and lift off the handle.

2 Remove the escutcheon cap. Remove cartridge mounting screws, and lift out the cylinder.

3 Remove the neoprene seals from the cylinder openings.

4 Clean the cylinder openings and the neoprene seals with an abrasive pad. Rinse cylinder with clear water.

5 Return seals to the cylinder openings, and reassemble faucet. Move handle to ON position, then slowly open shutoff valves. When water runs steadily, close faucet.

Install a new cylinder only if the faucet continues to leak after cleaning.

Sprayer head

Handle mount

Sprayer base

Distance between tailpieces (on-center)

Faucet sprayer nipple

Sprayer hose

Tailpiece

Mounting nut

Coupling nut

Supply tube

Shutoff valve

Replacing a Sink Faucet

Installing a new faucet is an easy project that takes about one hour. Before buying a new faucet, first find the diameter of the sink openings, and then measure the distance between the tailpieces (measured on-center). Make sure the tailpieces of the new faucet match the sink openings.

When shopping for a new faucet, choose a model made by a reputable manufacturer. Replacement parts for a well-known brand will be easy to find if the faucet ever needs repairs. Better faucets have solid brass bodies. They are easy to install and provide years of trouble-free service. Some washerless models have lifetime warranties.

Always install new supply tubes when replacing a faucet. Old supply tubes should not be reused.

Most codes accept the use of manufactured PB plastic supply tubes for exposed, undersink supply tubes. If water pipes underneath the sink do not have shutoff valves, you may choose to install the valves while replacing the faucet (pages 224 to 225).

Remember to turn off the water before beginning work (page 200).

Everything You Need

Tools: basin wrench or channel-type pliers, putty knife, caulk gun, adjustable wrenches.

Materials: penetrating oil, silicone caulk or plumber's putty, two flexible supply tubes.

1 Spray penetrating oil on tail-piece mounting nuts and supply tube coupling nuts. Remove the coupling nuts with a basin wrench or channel-type pliers.

2 Remove the tailpiece mounting nuts with a basin wrench or channel-type pliers. Basin wrench has a long handle that makes it easy to work in tight areas.

3 Remove faucet. Use a putty knife to clean away old putty from surface of sink.

Faucet Hookup Variations

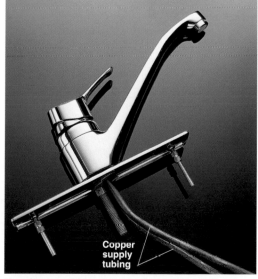

New faucet without supply tubes: Buy two supply tubes. Supply tubes are available in braided steel or vinyl mesh (shown above), PB plastic (acceptable by most codes for exposed supply lines), or chromed copper (page 224).

New faucet with preattached copper supply tubing: Make water connections by attaching the supply tubing directly to the shutoff valves with compression fittings (pages 52 to 53).

How to Install a New Sink Faucet

1 Apply a ¼" bead of silicone caulk or plumber's putty around the base of the faucet. Insert the faucet tailpieces into the sink openings. Position the faucet so base is parallel to back of sink, and press the faucet down to make sure caulk forms a good seal.

2 Screw the metal friction washers and the mounting nuts onto the tailpieces, then tighten with a basin wrench or channel-type pliers. Wipe away excess caulk around base of faucet.

3 Connect flexible supply tubes to faucet tailpieces. Tighten coupling nuts with a basin wrench or channel-type pliers.

4 Attach supply tubes to shut-off valves, using compression fittings (pages 52 to 53). Hand-tighten nuts, then use an adjustable wrench to tighten nuts ¼ turn. If necessary, hold valve with another wrench while tightening.

1 Attach faucet to sink by placing rubber gasket, retainer ring, and locknut onto threaded tailpiece. Tighten locknut with a basin wrench or channel-type pliers. Some center-mounted faucets have a decorative coverplate. Secure coverplate from underneath with washers and locknuts screwed onto coverplate bolts.

2 Connect preattached supply tubing to shutoff valves with compression fittings (pages 52 to 53). Red-coded tube should be attached to the hot water pipe, blue-coded tube to the cold water pipe.

How to Attach a Sink Sprayer

1 Apply a ¼" bead of plumber's putty or silicone caulk to bottom edge of sprayer base. Insert tailpiece of sprayer base into sink opening.

2 Place friction washer over tailpiece. Screw the mounting nut onto tailpiece and tighten with a basin wrench or channel-type pliers. Wipe away excess putty around base of sprayer.

3 Screw sprayer hose onto the hose nipple on the bottom of the faucet. Tighten ¼ turn, using a basin wrench or channel-type pliers.

223

Chromed
brass

CPVC
plastic

PB
plastic

Braided
steel

Chromed
copper

Vinyl
mesh

Shutoff valves allow you to shut off the water to an individual fixture so it can be repaired. They can be made from durable chromed brass or lightweight plastic. Shutoff valves come in ½" and ¾" diameters to match common water pipe sizes.

Supply tubes are used to connect water pipes to faucets, toilets, and other fixtures. They come in 12", 20", and 30" lengths. PB plastic and chromed copper tubes are inexpensive. Braided steel and vinyl mesh supply tubes are easy to install.

Installing Shutoff Valves & Supply Tubes

Worn-out shutoff valves or supply tubes can cause water to leak underneath a sink or other fixture. First, try tightening the fittings with an adjustable wrench. If this does not fix the leak, replace the shutoff valves and supply tubes.

Shutoff valves are available in several fitting types. For copper pipes, valves with compression-type fittings (pages 52 to 53) are easiest to install. For plastic pipes (pages 56 to 69), use grip-type valves. For galvanized iron pipes (pages 70 to 73), use valves with female threads.

Older plumbing systems often were installed without fixture shutoff valves. When repairing or replacing plumbing fixtures, you may want to install shutoff valves if they are not already present.

Everything You Need

Tools: hacksaw, tubing cutter, adjustable wrench, tubing bender, felt-tipped pen.

Materials: shutoff valves, supply tubes, pipe joint compound.

How to Install Shutoff Valves & Supply Tubes

Coupling
nut

Soldered
joints

Supply pipes

1 Turn off water at the main shutoff valve (page 12). Remove old supply pipes. If pipes are soldered copper, cut them off just below the soldered joint, using a hacksaw or tubing cutter. Make sure the cuts are straight. Unscrew the coupling nuts and discard the old pipes.

2 Slide a compression nut and compression ring over copper water pipe. Threads of nut should face end of pipe.

3 Apply pipe joint compound to the threads of the shutoff valve or compression nut. Screw the compression nut onto the shutoff valve and tighten with an adjustable wrench.

4 Bend chromed copper supply tube to reach from the tailpiece of the fixture to the shutoff valve, using a tubing bender (page 45). Bend the tube slowly to avoid kinking the metal.

5 Position the supply tube between fixture tailpiece and shutoff valve, and mark tube to length. Cut supply tube with a tubing cutter (page 47).

6 Attach bell-shaped end of supply tube to fixture tailpiece with coupling nut, then attach other end to shutoff valve with compression ring and nut (pages 52 to 53). Tighten all fittings with adjustable wrench.

225

Fixing Sprayers & Aerators

If water pressure from a sink sprayer seems low, or if water leaks from the handle, it is usually because lime buildup and sediment have blocked small openings inside the sprayer head. To fix the problem, first take the sprayer head apart and clean the parts. If cleaning the sprayer head does not help, the problem may be caused by a faulty diverter valve. The diverter valve inside the faucet body shifts water flow from the faucet spout to the sprayer when the sprayer handle is pressed. Cleaning or replacing the diverter valve may fix water pressure problems.

Whenever making repairs to a sink sprayer, check the sprayer hose for kinks or cracks. A damaged hose should be replaced.

If water pressure from a faucet spout seems low, or if the flow is partially blocked, take the spout aerator apart and clean the parts. The aerator is a screw-on attachment with a small wire screen that mixes tiny air bubbles into the water flow. Make sure the wire screen is not clogged with sediment and lime buildup. If water pressure is low throughout the house, it may be because galvanized iron water pipes are corroded. Corroded pipes should be replaced with copper (pages 44 to 51).

(pages 44 to 51)

Everything You Need

Tools: screwdriver, channel-type pliers, needlenose pliers, small brush.

Materials: vinegar, universal washer kit, heat-proof grease, replacement sprayer hose.

Clean faucet aerators and sink sprayers to fix most low water-pressure problems. Take aerator or sprayer head apart, then use a small brush dipped in vinegar to remove sediment.

Diverter valve

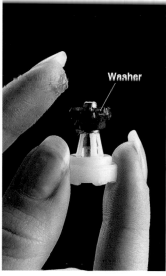

Washer

1 Shut off the water (page 208). Remove the faucet handle and the spout (see directions for your faucet type, pages 210 to 219).

2 Pull diverter valve from faucet body with needlenose pliers. Use a small brush dipped in vinegar to clean lime buildup and debris from valve.

3 Replace any worn O-rings or washers if possible. Coat the new parts with heatproof grease, then reinstall the diverter valve and reassemble the faucet.

How to Replace a Sprayer Hose

Faucet sprayer nipple

Sprayer hose

Washer

Handle mount

Retaining clip

Handle mount

1 Shut off the water. Unscrew sprayer hose from faucet sprayer nipple, using channel-type pliers. Pull sprayer hose through sink opening.

2 Unscrew the sprayer head from the handle mount. Remove washer.

3 Remove retaining clip with needlenose pliers; discard old hose. Attach handle mount, retaining clip, washer, and sprayer head to new hose. Attach sprayer hose to faucet sprayer nipple on faucet.

Tub & Shower Plumbing

Tub and shower faucets have the same basic designs as sink faucets, and the techniques for repairing leaks are the same as described in the faucet repair section of this book (pages 208 to 218). To identify your faucet design, you may have to take off the handle and disassemble the faucet.

When a tub and shower are combined, the showerhead and the tub spout share the same hot and cold water supply lines and handles. Combination faucets are available as three-handle, two-handle,

Tub & Shower Combination Faucets

Showerhead

Diverter valve

Cold water supply line

Hot water supply line

Tub spout

Three-handle faucet (pages 230 to 231) has valves that are either compression or cartridge design.

or single-handle types (below). The number of handles gives clues as to the design of the faucets and the kinds of repairs that may be necessary.

With combination faucets, a diverter valve or gate diverter is used to direct water flow to the tub spout or the showerhead. On three-handle faucet types, the middle handle controls a diverter valve. If water does not shift easily from tub to showerhead, or if water continues to run out the spout when the shower is on, the diverter valve probably needs to be cleaned and repaired (pages 230 to 231).

Two-handle and single-handle types use a gate diverter that is operated by a pull lever or knob on the tub spout. Although gate diverters rarely need repair, the lever occasionally may break, come loose, or refuse to stay in the UP position. To repair a gate diverter set in a tub spout, replace the entire spout (page 233).

Tub and shower faucets and diverter valves may be set inside wall cavities. Removing them may require a deep-set ratchet wrench (pages 231, 233).

If spray from the showerhead is uneven, clean the spray holes. If the showerhead does not stay in an upright position, remove the head and replace the O-ring (page 236).

To add a shower to an existing tub, install a flexible shower adapter (page 237). Several manufacturers make complete conversion kits that allow a shower to be installed in less than one hour.

Two-handle faucet (pages 232 to 233) has valves that are either compression or cartridge design.

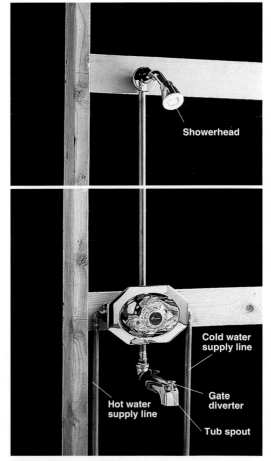

Single-handle faucet (pages 234 to 235) has valves that are cartridge, ball-type, or disc design.

Water line to
shower head

Diverter valve

Hot
water
supply
line

Cold
water
supply
line

Diverter
valve handle

Fixing Three-handle
Tub & Shower Faucets

A three-handle faucet type has two handles to control hot and cold water, and a third handle to control the diverter valve and direct water to either a tub spout or a shower head. The separate hot and cold handles indicate cartridge or compression faucet designs. To repair them, see pages 212 to 213 for cartridge, and 214 to 216 for compression.

If a diverter valve sticks, if water flow is weak, or if water runs out of the tub spout when the flow is directed to the showerhead, the diverter needs to be repaired or replaced. Most diverter valves are similar to either compression or cartridge faucet valves. Compression-type diverters can be repaired, but cartridge types should be replaced.

Remember to turn off the water (page 12) before beginning work.

Everything You Need

Tools: screwdriver, adjustable wrench or channel-type pliers, deep-set ratchet wrench, small wire brush.

Materials: replacement diverter cartridge or universal washer kit, heatproof grease, vinegar.

How to Repair a Compression Diverter Valve

Escutcheon

Diverter
handle

1 Remove the diverter valve handle with a screwdriver. Unscrew or pry off the escutcheon.

Bonnet nut

2 Remove bonnet nut with an adjustable wrench or channel-type pliers.

3 Unscrew the stem assembly, using a deep-set ratchet wrench. If necessary, chip away any mortar surrounding the bonnet nut (page 233, step 2).

Stem washer

Stem screw

Retaining nut

Threaded spindle

4 Remove brass stem screw. Replace stem washer with an exact duplicate. If stem screw is worn, replace it.

5 Unscrew threaded spindle from retaining nut.

6 Clean sediment and lime build-up from nut, using a small wire brush dipped in vinegar. Coat all parts with heatproof grease, and reassemble diverter valve.

Water line to shower head

Bonnet nut

Valve stem

Diverter lever

Cold water supply line

Gate diverter

Hot water supply line

Fixing Two-handle Tub & Shower Faucets

Two-handle tub and shower faucets are either cartridge or compression design. They may be repaired following the directions on pages 212 to 213 for cartridge, or pages 214 to 216 for compression. Because the valves of two-handle tub and shower faucets may be set inside the wall cavity, a deep-set socket wrench may be required to remove the valve stem.

Two-handle tub and shower designs have a gate diverter. A gate diverter is a simple mechanism located in the tub spout. A gate diverter closes the supply of water to the tub spout and redirects the flow to the shower head. Gate diverters seldom need repair. Occasionally, the lever may break, come loose, or refuse to stay in the UP position.

If the diverter fails to work properly, replace the tub spout. Tub spouts are inexpensive and easy to replace.

Remember to turn off the water (page 12) before beginning work.

Everything You Need

Tools: screwdriver, Allen wrench, pipe wrench, channel-type pliers, small cold chisel, ball-peen hammer, deep-set ratchet wrench.

Materials: masking tape or cloth, pipe joint compound, replacement faucet parts, as needed.

Check underneath tub spout for a small access slot. The slot indicates the spout is held in place with an Allen screw. Remove the screw, using an Allen wrench. Spout will slide off.

Unscrew faucet spout. Use a pipe wrench, or insert a large screwdriver or hammer handle into the spout opening and turn spout counterclockwise.

Spread pipe joint compound on threads of spout nipple before replacing spout.

How to Remove a Deep-set Faucet Valve

1 Remove handle and unscrew the escutcheon with channel-type pliers. Pad the jaws of the pliers with masking tape to prevent scratching the escutcheon.

2 Chip away any mortar surrounding the bonnet nut, using a ball-peen hammer and a small cold chisel.

3 Unscrew the bonnet nut with a deep-set ratchet wrench. Remove the bonnet nut and stem from the faucet body.

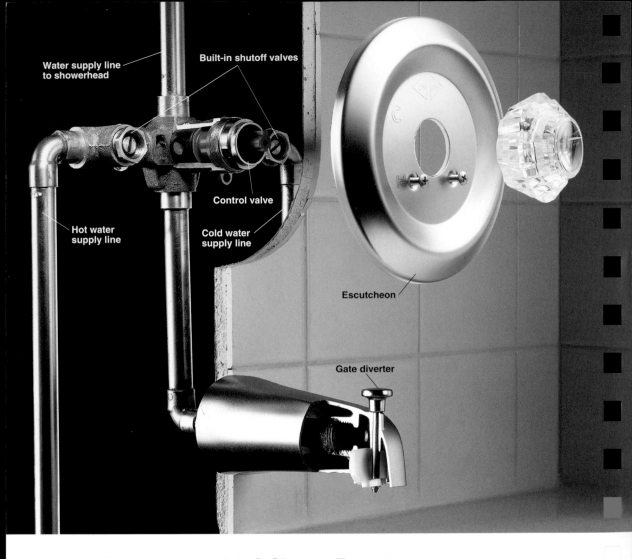

Water supply line to showerhead

Built-in shutoff valves

Hot water supply line

Control valve

Cold water supply line

Escutcheon

Gate diverter

Fixing Single-handle Tub & Shower Faucets

A single-handle tub and shower faucet has one valve that controls both water flow and temperature. Single-handle faucets may be ball-type, cartridge, or disc designs.

If a single-handle control valve leaks or does not function properly, disassemble the faucet, clean the valve, and replace any worn parts. Use the repair techniques described on pages 210 to 211 for ball-type, or pages 218 to 219 for ceramic disc. Repairing a single-handle cartridge faucet is shown on the opposite page.

Direction of the water flow to either the tub spout or the showerhead is controlled by a gate

diverter. Gate diverters seldom need repair. Occasionally, the lever may break, come loose, or refuse to stay in the UP position. If the diverter fails to work properly, replace the tub spout (page 233).

Everything You Need

Tools: screwdriver, adjustable wrench, channel-type pliers.

Materials: replacement faucet parts, as needed.

How to Repair a Single-handle Cartridge Tub & Shower Faucet

1 Use a screwdriver to remove the handle and escutcheon.

2 Turn off water supply at built-in shutoff valves or main shutoff valve (page 12).

3 Unscrew and remove retaining ring or bonnet nut, using an adjustable wrench.

4 Remove cartridge assembly by grasping end of valve with channel-type pliers and pulling gently.

5 Flush valve body with clean water to remove sediment. Replace any worn O-rings. Reinstall cartridge and test valve. If faucet fails to work properly, replace the cartridge.

Shower arm

Collar nut

Swivel ball nut

Spray adjustment cam lever

Swivel ball

O-ring

Spray outlets

Fixing & Replacing Showerheads

If spray from the showerhead is uneven, clean the spray holes. The outlet or inlet holes of the showerhead may get clogged with mineral deposits. Showerheads pivot into different positions. If a showerhead does not stay in position, or if it leaks, replace the O-ring that seals against the swivel ball.

A tub can be equipped with a shower by installing a flexible shower adapter kit. Complete kits are available at hardware stores and home centers.

Everything You Need

Tools: adjustable wrench or channel-type pliers, pipe wrench, drill, glass & tile bit (if needed), mallet, screwdriver.

Materials: masking tape, thin wire (paper clip), heatproof grease, rag, replacement O-rings (if needed), masonry anchors, flexible shower adapter kit (optional).

A typical showerhead can be disassembled easily for cleaning and repair. Some showerheads include a spray adjustment cam lever that is used to change the force of the spray.

How to Clean & Repair a Showerhead

Swivel ball nut

Collar nut

Inlet holes

O-ring

1 Unscrew the swivel ball nut, using an adjustable wrench or channel-type pliers. Wrap jaws of the tool with masking tape to prevent marring the finish. Unscrew collar nut from the showerhead.

2 Clean outlet and inlet holes of showerhead with a thin wire. Flush the head with clean water.

3 Replace the O-ring, if necessary. Lubricate the O-ring with heatproof grease before installing.

How to Install a Flexible Shower Adapter

1 Remove old tub spout (page 233). Install new tub spout from kit, using a pipe wrench. New spout will have an adapter hose outlet. Wrap the tub spout with a rag to prevent damage to the chrome finish.

2 Attach flexible shower hose to the adaptor hose outlet. Tighten with an adjustable wrench or channel-type pliers.

3 Determine location of shower-head hanger. Use hose length as a guide, and make sure shower-head can be easily lifted off hanger.

4 Mark hole locations. Use a glass and tile bit to drill holes in ceramic tile for masonry anchors.

5 Insert anchors into holes, and tap into place with a wooden or rubber mallet.

6 Fasten showerhead holder to the wall, and hang showerhead.

237

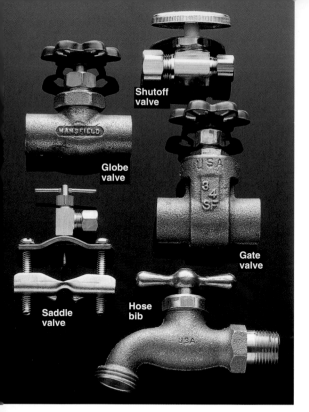

Shutoff valve

Globe valve

Gate valve

Saddle valve

Hose bib

Repairing Valves & Hose Bibs

Valves make it possible to shut off water at any point in the supply system. If a pipe breaks or a plumbing fixture begins to leak, you can shut off water to the damaged area so that it can be repaired. A hose bib is a faucet with a threaded spout, often used to connect rubber utility or appliance hoses.

Valves and hose bibs leak when washers or seals wear out. Replacement parts can be found in the same universal washer kits used to repair compression faucets (page 214). Coat replacement washers with heatproof grease to keep them soft and prevent cracking.

Remember to turn off the water before beginning work (page 12).

Everything You Need

Tools: screwdriver, adjustable wrench.

Materials: universal washer kit, heatproof grease.

How to Fix a Leaky Hose Bib

Packing nut

1 Remove the handle screw, and lift off the handle. Unscrew the packing nut with an adjustable wrench.

Handle screw

Handle

Packing nut

Packing washer

Spindle

Packing ring

Stem washer

Stem screw

2 Unscrew the spindle from the valve body. Remove the stem screw and replace the stem washer. Replace the packing washer, and reassemble the valve.

Gate valve has a movable brass wedge, or "gate," that screws up and down to control water flow. Gate valves may develop leaks around the handle. Repair leaks by replacing the packing washer or packing string found underneath the packing nut (page 215).

Globe valve has a curved chamber. Repair leaks around the handle by replacing the packing washer. If valve does not fully stop water flow when closed, replace the stem washer.

Shutoff valve controls water supply to one or more fixtures (pages 224 to 225). A shutoff valve has a plastic spindle with a packing washer and a snap-on stem washer. Repair leaks around the handle by replacing the packing washer. If a valve does not fully stop water flow when closed, replace the stem washer. Shutoff valves with multiple outlets are available to supply several fixtures from a single supply.

Saddle valve is a small fitting often specified to connect a refrigerator icemaker or sink-mounted water filter to copper pipe. A saddle valve contains a hollow spike that punctures water pipe when valve is first closed. The fitting is sealed with a rubber gasket. Some codes prohibit their use. A dual-outlet shutoff valve or a T-fitting are better substitutes.

239

Anti-siphon device

Rim joist

Stem seal

Stem

Lap siding

Sheathing

Frost-proof sillcock is mounted against the rim joist (sill) and has a long stem that reaches 6" to 30" inside the house to protect the valve from cold. A sillcock should angle downward slightly from the main toward the sill to provide drainage. The stem washer and O-ring (or packing string) can be replaced if the sillcock begins to

Installing & Repairing Sillcocks

A sillcock is a compression faucet attached to the outside of the house. Repair a leaky sillcock by replacing the stem washer and the O-ring.

Sillcocks can be damaged by frost. To repair a ruptured pipe, see pages 292 to 293. To prevent pipes from rupturing, close the indoor shutoff valve at the start of the cold weather season, disconnect all garden hoses, and open the sillcock to let trapped water drain out.

A special frost-proof sillcock has a long stem that reaches at least 6" inside the house to protect it from cold. Install a sillcock so the pipe angles downward from the shutoff valve. This allows water to drain away each time the faucet is turned off.

Remember to turn off the water before beginning work (page 12).

Everything You Need

Tools: screwdriver, channel-type pliers, pencil, right-angle drill or standard drill, 1" spade bit, caulk gun, hacksaw or tubing cutter, propane torch.

Materials: universal washer kit, sillcock, silicone caulk, 2" corrosion-resistant screws, copper pipe, T-fitting, Teflon tape, threaded adapter, shutoff valve, emery cloth, soldering paste (flux), solder.

How to Repair a Sillcock

Retaining nut

Stem

O-ring

1 Remove sillcock handle, and loosen retaining nut with channel-type pliers. Remove stem. Replace O-ring found on retaining nut or stem.

Washer

Stem screw

2 Remove the brass stem screw at the end of the stem, and replace the washer. Reassemble the sillcock.

Stem washer & valve seat

Globe style shut-off valve

Threaded adapter

Bleed screw

leak. In a copper plumbing system, the sillcock is connected to a nearby cold water supply pipe with a threaded adapter, two lengths of soldered copper pipe, and a shutoff valve. A T-fitting (not shown) is used to tap into an existing cold water pipe.

How to Install a Frost-proof Sillcock

Rim joist

1 Locate position of hole for sillcock. From nearest cold water pipe, mark a point on rim joist that is slightly lower than water pipe. Drill a hole through the joist, sheathing, and siding, using a 1" spade bit.

Sillcock flange

Caulk

2 Apply a thick bead of silicone caulk to bottom of sillcock flange, then insert sillcock into hole, and attach to siding with 2" corrosion-resistant screws. Turn handle to ON position. Wipe away excess caulk.

T-fitting

End of sillcock

3 Mark cold water pipe, then cut pipe and install a T-fitting (pages 40, 48 to 50). Wrap Teflon tape around threads of sillcock.

Copper pipe

Threaded adapter

Sillcock

Shutoff valve

Teflon tape

4 Join T-fitting to sillcock with threaded adapter (page 43), a shutoff valve, and two lengths of copper pipe. Prepare pipes and solder the joints. Turn on water, and close sillcock when water runs steadily.

(8) Float ball

(1) Handle

(2) Flapper (or tank ball)

Lift chain (or lift wires)

Tank

(7) Ballcock

Rim openings

(3) Flush valve

(4) Toilet bowl

Supply tube

(5) Trap

Base

Shutoff valve

Wax ring

(6) Main drain

How a toilet works: When the handle (1) is pushed, the lift chain raises a rubber seal, called a **flapper, or tank ball (2)**. Water in the tank rushes down through the **flush valve opening (3)** in the bottom of the tank, into the **toilet bowl (4)**. Waste water in the bowl is forced through the **trap (5)** into the **main drain (6)**.

When the toilet tank is empty, the flapper seals the tank, and a water supply valve, called a **ballcock (7)**, refills the toilet tank. The ballcock is controlled by a **float ball (8)** that rides on the surface of the water. When the tank is full, the float ball automatically shuts off the ballcock.

Common Toilet Problems

A clogged toilet is one of the most common plumbing problems. If a toilet overflows or flushes sluggishly, clear the clog with a plunger or closet auger (page 260). If the problem persists, the clog may be in the main waste-vent stack (page 267).

Most other toilet problems are fixed easily with minor adjustments that require no disassembly or replacement parts. You can make these adjustments in a few minutes, using simple tools (page 244).

If minor adjustments do not fix the problem, further repairs will be needed. The parts of a standard toilet are not difficult to take apart, and most repair projects can be completed in less than an hour.

A recurring puddle of water on the floor around a toilet may be caused by a crack in the toilet base or in the tank. A damaged toilet should be replaced. Installing a new toilet is an easy project that can be finished in three or four hours.

A standard two-piece toilet has an upper tank that is bolted to a base. This type of toilet uses a simple gravity-operated flush system and can be repaired easily using the directions on the following pages. Some one-piece toilets use a complicated, high-pressure flush valve. High-pressure toilets can be adjusted, but replacing valves should be done by a professional.

Problems	Repairs
Toilet handle sticks or is hard to push.	1. Adjust lift wires (page 244). 2. Clean & adjust handle (page 244).
Handle is loose.	1. Adjust handle (page 244). 2. Reattach lift chain or lift wires to lever (page 244).
Toilet will not flush at all.	1. Make sure water is turned on. 2. Adjust lift chain or lift wires (page 244).
Toilet does not flush completely.	1. Adjust lift chain (page 244). 2. Adjust water level in tank (page 246). 3. Increase pressure on pressure-assisted toilet (page 252).
Toilet overflows or flushes sluggishly.	1. Clear clogged toilet (page 260). 2. Clear clogged main waste-vent stack (page 267).
Toilet runs continuously.	1. Adjust lift wires or lift chain (page 244). 2. Replace leaky float ball (page 245). 3. Adjust water level in tank (page 246). 4. Adjust and clean flush valve (page 249). 5. Replace flush valve (page 249). 6. Repair or replace ballcock (pages 246 to 247). 7. Service pressure-assist valve (page 253).
Water on floor around toilet.	1. Tighten tank bolts and water connections (page 250). 2. Insulate tank to prevent condensation (page 250). 3. Replace wax ring (page 251). 4. Replace cracked tank or bowl (pages 250 to 251).

Making Minor Adjustments

Many common toilet problems can be fixed by making minor adjustments to the handle and the attached lift chain (or lift wires).

If the handle sticks or is hard to push, remove the tank cover and clean the handle mounting nut. Make sure the lift wires are straight.

If the toilet will not flush completely unless the handle is held down, you may have to remove excess slack in the lift chain.

If the toilet will not flush at all, the lift chain may be broken or may have to be reattached to the handle lever.

A continuously running toilet (page opposite) can be caused by bent lift wires, kinks in a lift chain, or lime buildup on the handle mounting nut. Clean and adjust the handle and the lift wires or chain to fix the problem.

Everything You Need
Tools: adjustable wrench, needlenose pliers, screwdriver, small wire brush.
Materials: vinegar.

How to Adjust a Toilet Handle & Lift Chain (or Lift Wires)

Clean and adjust handle mounting nut so handle operates smoothly. Mounting nut has reversed threads. Loosen nut by turning clockwise; tighten by turning counterclockwise. Remove lime buildup with a brush dipped in vinegar.

Adjust lift chain so it hangs straight from handle lever, with about ½" of slack. Remove excess slack in chain by hooking the chain in a different hole in the handle lever or by removing links with needlenose pliers. A broken lift chain must be replaced.

Adjust lift wires (found on toilets without lift chains) so that wires are straight and operate smoothly when handle is pushed. A sticky handle often can be fixed by straightening bent lift wires.

Fixing a Running Toilet

The sound of continuously run-ning water occurs if fresh water continues to enter the toilet tank after the flush cycle is complete. A running toilet can waste 20 or more gallons of fresh water each day.

To fix a running toilet, first jiggle the toilet handle. If the sound of running water stops, then either the handle or the lift wires (or lift chain) need to be adjusted (page opposite).

If the sound of running water does not stop when the handle is jiggled, then remove the tank cover and check to see if the float ball is touching the side of the tank. If necessary, bend the float arm to reposition the float ball away from the side of the tank. Make sure the float ball is not leaking. To check for leaks, unscrew the float ball and shake it gently. If there is water inside the ball, replace it.

If these minor adjustments do not fix the problem, then you will have to adjust or repair the ballcock or the flush valve (photo, right). Follow the direc-tions on the following pages.

Everything You Need

Tools: screwdriver, small wire brush, sponge, adjustable wrenches, spud wrench or channel-type pliers.

Materials: universal washer kit, ballcock (if needed), ballcock seals, emery cloth, fiber abra-sive pad, flapper or tank ball, flush valve (if needed).

The sound of continuously running water can be caused by several different problems: the **lift wire (1)** (or lift chain) is bent or kinked; the **float ball (2)** leaks or rubs against the side of the tank; a faulty **ballcock (3)** does not shut off the fresh water supply; or the **flush valve (4)** allows water to leak down into the toilet bowl. First, check the lift wires and float ball. If making simple adjustments and repairs to these parts does not fix the problem, then you will have to repair the ballcock or flush valve (photo, below).

Check the overflow pipe if the sound of running water continues after the float ball and lift wires are adjusted. If you see **water flowing into the overflow pipe**, the ballcock must be repaired. First adjust ballcock to lower the water level in the tank (page 246). If problem continues, repair or replace the ballcock (pages 247 to 248). If **water is not flowing into the overflow pipe**, then the flush valve must be repaired (page 249). First check the tank ball (or flapper) for wear, and replace if necessary. If problem continues, replace the flush valve.

How to Adjust a Ballcock to Set Water Level

Traditional plunger-valve ballcock is made of brass. Water flow is controlled by a plunger attached to the float arm and ball. Lower the water level by bending the float arm downward slightly. Raise the water level by bending float arm upward.

Diaphragm ballcock usually is made of plastic and has a wide bonnet that contains a rubber diaphragm. Turn the adjustment screw clockwise to raise the water level. Turn it counterclockwise to lower the water level. Bend the float arm to make larger adjustments, if necessary.

Float cup ballcock is made of plastic and is easy to adjust. Lower the water level by pinching spring clip on pull rod and moving float cup downward on the ballcock shank. Raise the water level by moving the cup upward.

Floatless ballcock controls water level with a pressure-sensing device. Turn the adjustment screw clockwise, ½ turn at a time, to raise the water level; counterclockwise to lower it. NOTE: Floatless ballcocks are no longer allowed by code and should be replaced.

How to Repair a Plunger-valve Ballcock

1 Shut off the water, and flush to empty the tank. Remove the wing nuts on the ballcock. Slip out the float arm.

2 Pull up on the plunger to remove it. Pry out packing washer or O-ring. Pry out plunger washer. (Remove stem screw, if necessary.)

3 Install replacement washers. Clean sediment from inside of ballcock with a wire brush. Reassemble ballcock.

How to Repair a Diaphragm Ballcock

1 Shut off the water, and flush to empty the tank. Remove the screws from the bonnet.

2 Lift off float arm with bonnet attached. Check diaphragm and plunger for wear.

3 Replace any stiff or cracked parts. If assembly is badly worn, replace the entire ballcock (page 248).

How to Repair a Float Cup Ballcock

1 Shut off the water, and flush to empty the tank. Remove the ballcock cap.

2 Remove bonnet by pushing down on shaft and turning counterclockwise. Clean out sediment inside ballcock with wire brush.

3 Replace the seal. If assembly is badly worn, replace the entire ballcock (page 248).

How to Install a New Ballcock

1 Shut off water, and flush toilet to empty tank. Use a sponge to remove remaining water. Disconnect supply tube coupling nut and ball-cock mounting nut with adjustable wrench. Remove old ballcock.

2 Loosen the shank locking on the new ballcock. Adjust the shank until the top of the ballcock is 1" from the top of the tank. Tighten the locking.

3 Attach a cone washer to the new ballcock, and insert the tailpiece into the tank opening.

4 Screw in the float arm and align it so it passes in front of the overflow pipe. Screw on the float ball. Position the refill tube so it fits inside the overflow pipe.

5 Screw the mounting nut and the supply tube coupling nut onto ballcock tailpiece. Tighten them. Turn on the water and check for leaks.

How to Adjust & Clean a Flush Valve

Adjust tank ball (or flapper) so it is directly over flush valve. Tank ball has a guide arm that can be loosened so that tank ball can be repositioned. (Some tank balls have a ball guide that helps seat the tank ball into the flush valve.)

Replace the tank ball if it is cracked or worn. Tank balls have a threaded fitting that screws onto the lift wire. Clean opening of the flush valve, using emery cloth (for brass valves) or a fiber abrasive pad (for plastic valves).

Replace flapper if it is worn. Flappers are attached to small lugs on the sides of overflow pipe.

How to Install a New Flush Valve

1 Shut off water, disconnect ball-cock (page opposite, step 1), and remove toilet tank (page 251, steps 1 and 2). Remove old flush valve by unscrewing spud nut with spud wrench or channel-type pliers.

2 Slide cone washer onto tailpiece of new flush valve. Beveled side of cone washer should face end of tailpiece. Insert flush valve into tank opening so that overflow pipe faces ballcock.

3 Screw spud nut onto tailpiece of flush valve, and tighten with a spud wrench or channel-type pliers. Place soft spud washer over tailpiece, and reinstall toilet tank.

Toilet base

Wax ring

Toilet flange

Horn

Rubber sleeve

Subfloor

Drain

Fixing a Leaking Toilet

Water leaking onto the floor around a toilet may be caused by several different problems. The leaking must be fixed as soon as possible to prevent moisture from damaging the subfloor.

First, make sure all connections are tight. If moisture drips from the tank during humid weather, it is probably condensation. Fix this "sweating" problem by insulating the inside of the tank with foam panels. A crack in a toilet tank also can cause leaks. A cracked tank must be replaced.

Water seeping around the base of a toilet can be caused by an old wax ring that no longer seals against the drain (photo, above), or by a cracked toilet base. If leaking occurs during or just after a flush, replace the wax ring. If leaking is constant,

the toilet base is cracked and must be replaced. New toilets usually are sold with flush valves and ballcocks already installed. If these parts are not included, you will have to purchase them.

Building codes require the installation of 1.6-gallon low-flow toilets in all new construction and bathroom remodeling projects. Refer to page 130 to 131 for toilet installation.

Everything You Need:

Tools: sponge, adjustable wrench, putty knife, ratchet wrench, screwdriver.

Materials: tank liner kit, abrasive cleanser, rag, wax ring, plumber's putty.

Ballcock mounting nut

Supply tube coupling nut

Tank bolt

Tighten all connections slightly. Tighten nuts on tank bolts with a ratchet wrench. Tighten ballcock mounting nut and supply tube coupling nut with an adjustable wrench. **Caution: overtightening tank bolts may crack the toilet tank.**

Insulate toilet tank to prevent "sweating," using a toilet liner kit. First, shut off water, drain tank, and clean inside of tank with abrasive cleanser. Cut plastic foam panels to fit bottom, sides, front, and back of tank. Attach panels to tank with adhesive (included in kit). Let adhesive cure as directed.

1 Turn off water, and flush to empty toilet tank. Use a sponge to remove remaining water in tank and bowl. Disconnect supply tube with an adjustable wrench.

2 Remove the nuts from the tank bolts with a ratchet wrench. Carefully remove the tank and set it aside.

3 Pry off the floor bolt trim caps at the base of the toilet. Remove the floor nuts with an adjustable wrench.

4 Straddle the toilet and rock the bowl from side to side until the seal breaks. Carefully lift the toilet off the floor bolts and set it on its side. Small amount of water may spill from the toilet trap.

5 Remove old wax from the toilet flange in the floor. Plug the drain opening with a damp rag to prevent sewer gases from rising into the house.

6 If old toilet will be reused, clean old wax and putty from the horn and the base of the toilet. NOTE: Refer to pages 130 to 131 for toilet installation.

Flush handle

Air inducer

Vacuum breaker

Flush valve assembly

Pressure tank

Discharge extension

Pressure relief valve

Supply shank

Pressure-assisted toilets rely on pressure rather than water volume to create an adequate flush. The handle is connected to a flush rod that pushes an actuator on the flush valve cartridge to start the flush.

Fixing a Pressure-assisted Toilet

Pressure-assisted toilets develop problems similar to those of conventional toilets, such as continuously running water and a weak flush. And while the causes may be different, the repairs are just as easy.

Pressure-assisted toilets require a certain level of water-pressure—between 20 and 80 psi—to work properly. Pressure below that level can cause a variety of problems; if you're having trouble with a pressure-assisted toilet, the first thing to check is your home's water pressure.

If the system's pressure is sufficient, clean the water intake screen to ensure maximum flow into the tank. If the pressure is weak, call a plumber or your water utility for advice.

Before making any repairs to your pressure-assisted toilet, turn off the water at the fixture shut-off valve and flush the toilet to relieve the pressure in the tank.

Everything You Need
Tools: adjustable wrench, soft brush, channel-type pliers.
Materials: 5-gallon bucket.

How to Test & Improve Water Pressure

1 Turn off the water at the shutoff valve and flush the toilet. Use an adjustable wrench or channel-type pliers to loosen the coupling nut connecting the water supply tube to the supply shank at the bottom of the tank.

2 Place the free end of the supply tube into a 5-gallon bucket. Mark the time, then open the shut-off valve all the way for 30 seconds. Close the valve and measure the amount of water: there should be more than a gallon.

Supply assembly

Screen

3 Place a bucket under the supply shank. Remove the shank mounting nut, and pull the supply assembly from the tank hole. Inspect the screen inside the shank, and clean it with a soft brush. Reconnect the shank and supply tube.

1 Turn off water at the shutoff valve, and flush the toilet. Lift up on the flush rod: there should be a ⅛" gap between the rod and the top of the actuator. To adjust, loosen the setscrew and rotate the actuator up or down.

2 Unscrew the flush valve cartridge, using the handle ends of channel-type pliers.

3 Inspect the O-rings. If they are worn, replace the cartridge. Reinstall the cartridge, and tighten it. Restore the water supply and let the tank refill. If water runs after refill, depress the actuator. If the flow stops, tighten the cartridge in quarter-turns until the water stops; if flow continues, loosen the cartridge until the water stops.

How to Correct a Weak Flow

1 With the water supply on, flush the toilet by depressing the actuator. Once the unit begins the flush cycle, carefully raise the actuator. This flushes the system with water to remove debris.

2 Test the air inducer. Remove the inducer cap, and flush the toilet. Look inside the inducer to make sure that the plastic poppet retracts, and listen for air flow. If there is no flow, unscrew the inducer, and clean the inducer, poppet, spring, and cap.

3 Test for a leaking flush valve cartridge. Turn off the water at the shutoff valve, and flush the toilet. Pour a cup of water into the top of the cartridge, then restore the water supply. If you see a stream of bubbles rising from the cartridge, replace it.

Clearing Clogs & Fixing Drains

Clear a clogged drain with a plunger, hand auger, or blow bag. A plunger breaks up clogs by forcing air pressure into the drain line. Because a plunger is effective and simple to use, it should be the first choice for clearing a clog.

A hand auger has a flexible steel cable that is pushed into the drain line to break up or remove obstructions. An auger is easy to use, but for best results the user must know the "feel" of the cable in the drain line. A little experience often is necessary to tell the difference between a soap clog and a bend in the drain line (pages 258 to 261).

A blow bag hooks to a garden hose and uses water pressure to clear clogs. Blow bags are most effective on clogs in floor drains (page 265).

Use caustic, acid-based chemical drain cleaners only as a last resort. These drain cleaners, usually available at hardware stores and supermarkets, will dissolve clogs, but they also may damage pipes and must be handled with caution. Always read the manufacturer's directions completely.

Regular maintenance helps keep drains working properly. Flush drains once each week with hot tap water to keep them free of soap, grease, and debris. Or, treat drains once every six months with a non-caustic (copper sulfide- or sodium hydroxide-based) drain cleaner. A non-caustic cleaner will not harm pipes.

Occasionally, leaks may occur in the drain lines or around the drain opening. Most leaks in drain lines are fixed easily by gently tightening all pipe connections. If the leak is at the sink drain opening, fix or replace the strainer body assembly (page 257).

Clearing Clogged Sinks

Every sink has a drain trap and a fixture drain line. Sink clogs usually are caused by a buildup of soap and hair in the trap or fixture drain line. Remove clogs by using a plunger, disconnecting and cleaning the trap (page 256), or using a hand auger (pages 258 to 259).

Many sinks hold water with a mechanical plug called a pop-up stopper. If the sink will not hold standing water, or if water in the sink drains too slowly, the pop-up stopper must be cleaned and adjusted (page 256).

Everything You Need

Tools: plunger, channel-type pliers, small wire brush, screwdriver.

Materials: rag, bucket, replacement gaskets.

Supply tubes
Clevis
Drain stopper pivot rod
Fixture drain line
Drain trap
Shutoff valve
Standing trap water

Drain trap holds water that seals the drain line and prevents sewer gases from entering the home. Each time a drain is used, the standing trap water is flushed away and replaced by new water. The shape of the trap and fixture drain line may resemble the letter P, and sink traps sometimes are called P-traps.

How to Clear Sink Drains with a Plunger

1 Remove drain stopper. Some pop-up stoppers lift out directly; others turn counterclockwise. On some older types of stoppers, the pivot rod must be removed to free the stopper.

2 Stuff a wet rag in sink overflow opening; rag prevents air from breaking the suction of the plunger. Place plunger cup over drain and run enough water to cover the rubber cup. Move plunger handle up and down rapidly to break up the clog.

How to Clean & Adjust a Pop-up Sink Drain Stopper

1 Raise stopper lever to full upright (closed) position. Unscrew the retaining nut that holds pivot rod in position. Pull pivot rod out of drain pipe to release stopper.

2 Remove stopper. Clean debris from stopper, using a small wire brush. Inspect gasket for wear or damage, and replace if necessary. Reinstall stopper.

3 If sink does not drain properly, adjust clevis. Loosen clevis screw. Slide clevis up or down on stopper rod to adjust position of stopper. Tighten clevis screw.

How to Remove & Clean a Sink Drain Trap

1 Place bucket under trap to catch water and debris. Loosen slip nuts on trap bend with channel-type pliers. Unscrew nuts by hand and slide away from connections. Pull off trap bend.

2 Dump out debris. Clean trap bend with a small wire brush. Inspect slip nut washers for wear, and replace if necessary. Reinstall trap bend, and tighten slip nuts.

Fixing Leaky Sink Strainers

A leak under a sink may be caused by a strainer body that is not properly sealed to the sink drain opening. To check for leaks, close the drain stopper and fill sink with water. From underneath sink, inspect the strainer assembly for leaks.

Remove the strainer body, clean it, and replace the gaskets and plumber's putty. Or, replace the strainer with a new one, available at home centers.

Everything You Need

Tools: channel-type pliers, spud wrench, hammer, putty knife.

Materials: plumber's putty, replacement parts (if needed).

Sink strainer assembly connects the sink to the drain line. Leaks may occur where the strainer body seals against the lip of the drain opening.

1 Unscrew slip nuts from both ends of tailpiece, using channel-type pliers. Disconnect tailpiece from strainer body and trap bend. Remove tailpiece.

2 Remove the locknut, using a spud wrench. Stubborn locknuts may be removed by tapping on the lugs with a hammer. Unscrew the locknut completely, and remove the strainer assembly. If necessary, cut the locknut.

3 Remove old putty from the drain opening, using a putty knife. If reusing the old strainer body, clean off old putty from under the flange. Old gaskets and washers should be replaced.

4 Apply a bead of plumber's putty to the lip of the drain opening. Press strainer body into drain opening. From under the sink, place rubber gasket, then metal or fiber friction ring, over strainer. Reinstall locknut and tighten. Reinstall tailpiece.

How to Clear a Fixture Drain Line with a Hand Auger

1 Remove trap bend (page 256). Push the end of the auger cable into the drain line opening until resistance is met. This resistance usually indicates end of cable has reached a bend in the drain pipe.

2 Set the auger lock so that at least 6" of cable extends out of the opening. Crank the auger handle in a clockwise direction to move the end of the cable past bend in drain line.

3 Release the lock and continue pushing the cable into the opening until firm resistance is felt. Set the auger lock and crank the handle in a clockwise direction. Solid resistance that prevents the cable from advancing indicates a clog. Some clogs, such as a sponge or an accumulation of hair, can be snagged and retrieved (step 4). Continuous resistance that allows the cable to advance slowly is probably a soap clog (step 5).

Hand grip

4 Pull an obstruction out of the line by releasing the auger lock and cranking the handle clockwise. If no object can be retrieved, reconnect the trap bend and use the auger to clear the nearest branch drain line or main waste and vent stack (pages 266 to 267).

5 Continuous resistance indicates a soap clog. Bore through the clog by cranking the auger handle clockwise, while applying steady pressure on the hand grip of the auger. Repeat the procedure two or three times, then retrieve the cable. Reconnect the trap bend and flush the system with hot tap water to remove debris.

Clearing Clogged Toilets

Most toilet clogs occur because an object is stuck inside the toilet trap. Use a flanged plunger or a closet auger to remove the clog.

A toilet that is sluggish during the flush cycle may be partially blocked. Clear the blockage with a plunger or closet auger. Occasionally, a sluggish toilet flush indicates a blocked waste-vent stack. Clear the stack as shown on page 267.

Everything You Need

Tools: flanged plunger, closet auger.

Materials: bucket.

Toilet drain system has a drain outlet at the bottom of the bowl and a built-in trap. The toilet drain is connected to a drain line and a main waste-vent stack.

How to Clear a Toilet with a Plunger

Place cup of flanged plunger over drain outlet opening. Plunge up and down rapidly. Slowly pour a bucket of water into bowl to flush debris through drain. If toilet does not drain, repeat plunging, or clear clog with a closet auger.

How to Clear a Toilet with a Closet Auger

Place the auger bend in the bottom of the drain opening, and push the auger cable into the trap. Crank the auger handle in a clockwise direction to snag obstruction. Continue cranking while retrieving the cable to pull the obstruction out of the trap.

Clearing Clogged Shower Drains

Shower drain clogs usually are caused by an accumulation of hair in the drain line. Remove the strainer cover and look for clogs in the drain opening (below). Some clogs are removed easily with a piece of stiff wire.

Stubborn clogs should be removed with a plunger or hand auger.

Everything You Need

Tools: screwdriver, flashlight, plunger, hand auger.

Materials: stiff wire.

Drain opening

Floor

Sloped floor

Drain line

Trap

Waste-vent stack

Shower drain system has a sloped floor, a drain opening, a trap, and a drain line that connects to a branch drain line or waste-vent stack.

How to Clear a Shower Drain

Strainer cover

Check for clogs by removing strainer cover, using a screwdriver. Use a flashlight to look for hair clogs in the drain opening. Use a stiff wire to clear shower drain of hair or to snag any obstructions.

Use a plunger to clear most shower drain clogs. Place the rubber cup over the drain opening. Pour enough water into the shower stall to cover the lip of the cup. Move plunger handle up and down rapidly.

Clear stubborn clogs in the shower drain with a hand auger. Use the auger as shown on pages 258 to 259.

Plunger-type tub drain has a hollow brass plug, called a *plunger*, that slides up and down inside the overflow drain to seal off the water flow. The plunger is moved by a trip lever and linkage that runs through the overflow drain.

Fixing Tub Drains

When water in the tub drains slowly or not at all, remove and inspect the drain assembly. Both plunger and pop-up type drain mechanisms catch hair and other debris that cause clogs.

If cleaning the drain assembly does not fix the problem, the tub drain line is clogged. Clear the line with a plunger or a hand auger. Always stuff a wet rag in the overflow drain opening before plunging the tub drain. The rag prevents air from breaking the suction of the plunger. When using an auger, always insert the cable down through the overflow drain opening.

If the tub will not hold water with the drain closed, or if the tub continues to drain slowly after the assembly has been cleaned, then the drain assembly needs adjustment. Remove the assembly, and follow the instructions on the opposite page.

Everything You Need

Tools: plunger, screwdriver, small wire brush, needlenose pliers, hand auger.

Materials: vinegar, heatproof grease, rag.

Pop-up tub drain has a rocker arm that pivots to open or close a metal drain stopper. The rocker arm is moved by a trip lever and linkage that runs through the overflow drain.

Clear a tub drain by running the auger cable through the overflow opening. First, remove the coverplate and carefully lift out the drain linkage (page opposite). Push auger cable into the opening until resistance is felt (pages 258 to 259). After using the auger, replace drain linkage. Open drain and run hot water through drain to flush out any debris.

How to Clean & Adjust a Plunger-type Tub Drain

1 Remove screws on coverplate. Carefully pull coverplate, linkage, and plunger from the overflow drain opening.

2 Clean linkage and plunger with a small wire brush dipped in vinegar. Lubricate assembly with heatproof grease.

3 Adjust drain flow and fix leaks by adjusting linkage. Unscrew locknut on threaded lift rod, using needlenose pliers. Screw rod down about ⅛". Tighten locknut and reinstall entire assembly.

How to Clean & Adjust a Pop-up Tub Drain

1 Raise trip lever to the full open position. Carefully pull stopper and rocker arm assembly from drain opening. Clean hair or debris from rocker arm with a small wire brush.

2 Remove screws from coverplate. Pull coverplate, trip lever, and linkage from overflow drain. Remove hair and debris. Remove corrosion with a small wire brush dipped in vinegar. Lubricate linkage with heatproof grease.

3 Adjust drain flow and fix leaks by adjusting the linkage. Loosen locknut on threaded lift rod and screw lift rod up about ⅛". Tighten locknut and reinstall entire assembly.

Clearing Clogged Drum Traps

Labels on image:
Cover
Line in from tub
Line in from sink
Line out to toilet drain line

In older homes, clogs in bathroom sinks or bathtubs may be caused by blockage in the drain lines connected to a drum trap. Remove the drum trap cover and use a hand auger to clear each drain line.

Drum traps usually are located in the floor next to the bathtub. They are identified by a flat, screw-in type cover or plug that is flush with the floor. Occasionally, a drum trap will be positioned upside down so that the plug is accessible from below.

A drum trap is a canister made of lead or cast iron. Usually, more than one fixture drain line is connected to the drum. Drum traps are not vented, and they are no longer approved for new plumbing installations.

Everything You Need

Tools: adjustable wrench, hand auger.

Materials: rags or towels, penetrating oil, Teflon tape.

How to Clear a Clogged Drum Trap

1 Place rags or towels around the opening of the drum trap to absorb water that may be backed up in the lines.

2 Remove the trap cover, using an adjustable wrench. Work carefully: older drum traps may be made of lead, which gets brittle with age. If cover does not unscrew easily, apply penetrating oil to lubricate the threads.

3 Use a hand auger (pages 258 to 259) to clear each drain line. Then wrap the threads of the cover with Teflon tape and install. Flush all drains with hot water for five minutes.

Clearing Clogged Floor Drains

When water backs up onto a basement floor, there is a clog in either the floor drain line, drain trap, or the sewer service line. Clogs in the drain line or trap may be cleared with a hand auger or a blow bag. To clear a sewer service line, see pages 266 to 267.

Blow bags are especially useful for clearing clogs in floor drain lines. A blow bag attaches to a garden hose and is inserted directly into the floor drain line. The bag fills with water and then releases a powerful spurt that dislodges clogs.

Everything You Need

Tools: adjustable wrench, screwdriver, hand auger, blow bag.

Materials: garden hose.

Clear clogged floor drains using a hand auger. Remove the drain cover, then use a wrench to unscrew the cleanout plug in the drain bowl. Push the auger cable through the cleanout opening directly into the drain line.

How to Use a Blow Bag to Clear a Floor Drain

1 Attach blow bag to garden hose, then attach hose to a hose bib or utility faucet.

2 Remove drain cover and cleanout plug. Insert the blow bag completely into the cleanout opening and turn on water. Allow several minutes for the blow bag to work properly.

Clearing Clogs in Branch & Main Drain Lines

If using a plunger or a hand auger does not clear a clog in a fixture drain line, it means that the blockage may be in a branch line, the main waste-vent stack, or the sewer service line (see the photo on page 13).

First, use an auger to clear the branch drain line closest to any stopped-up fixtures. Branch drain lines may be serviced through the cleanout fittings located at the end of the branch. Because waste water may be backed up in the drain lines, always open a cleanout with caution. Place a bucket and rags under the opening to catch waste water. Never position yourself directly under a cleanout opening while unscrewing the plug or cover.

If using an auger on the branch line does not solve the problem, then the clog may be located in a main waste-vent stack. To clear the stack, run an auger cable down through the roof vent. Make sure that the cable of your auger is long enough to reach down the entire length of the stack. If it is not, you may want to rent or borrow another auger. Always use extreme caution when working on a ladder or on a roof.

If no clog is present in the main stack, the problem may be located in the sewer service line. Locate the main cleanout, usually a Y-shaped fitting at the bottom of the main waste-vent stack. Remove the plug and push the cable of a hand auger into the opening.

Some sewer service lines in older homes have a house trap. The house trap is a U-shaped fitting located at the point where the sewer line exits the house. Most of the fitting will be beneath the floor surface, but it can be identified by its two openings. Use a hand auger to clean a house trap.

If the auger meets solid resistance in the sewer line, retrieve the cable and inspect the bit. Fine, hair-like roots on the bit indicate the line is clogged with tree roots. Dirt on the bit indicates a collapsed line.

Use a power auger to clear sewer service lines that are clogged with tree roots. Power augers (page 37) are available at rental centers. However, a power auger is a large, heavy piece of equipment. Before renting, consider the cost of rental and the level of your do-it-yourself skills versus the price of a professional sewer cleaning service. If you rent a power auger, ask the rental dealer for complete instructions on how to operate the equipment.

Always consult a professional sewer cleaning service if you suspect a collapsed line.

Everything You Need

Tools: adjustable wrench or pipe wrench, hand auger, cold chisel, ball-peen hammer.

Materials: bucket, rags, penetrating oil, cleanout plug (if needed), pipe joint compound.

Clear a branch drain line by locating the cleanout fitting at the end of the line. Place a bucket underneath the opening to catch waste water, then slowly unscrew the cleanout plug with an adjustable wrench. Clear clogs in the branch drain line with a hand auger (pages 258 to 259).

Clear the main waste and vent stack by running the cable of a hand auger down through the roof vent. Always use extreme caution while working on a ladder or roof.

Clear the house trap in a sewer service line using a hand auger. Slowly remove only the plug on the "street side" of the trap. If water seeps out the opening as the plug is removed, the clog is in the sewer line beyond the trap. If no water seeps out, auger the trap. If no clog is present in the trap, replace the street-side plug and remove the house-side plug. Use the auger to clear clogs located between the house trap and main stack.

How to Remove & Replace a Main Drain Cleanout Plug

1 Remove the cleanout plug, using a large wrench. If plug does not turn out, apply penetrating oil around edge of plug, wait 10 minutes, and try again. Place rags and a bucket under fitting opening to catch any water that may be backed up in the line.

2 Remove stubborn plugs by placing the cutting edge of chisel on edge of plug. Strike chisel with a ball-peen hammer to move plug counterclockwise. If plug does not turn out, break it into pieces with the chisel and hammer. Remove all broken pieces.

3 Replace old plug with new plastic plug. Apply pipe joint compound to the threads of the replacement plug and screw into cleanout fitting.

Alternate: Replace old plug with an expandable rubber plug. A wing nut squeezes the rubber core between two metal plates. The rubber bulges slightly to create a watertight seal.

Heat-saver
nipple fitting

Flue
hat

Flexible
water
connection

(1) Hot
water
outlet

Glass-
lined
tank

(2) Dip
tube

Pressure-
relief
valve

Anode
rod

Outer
jacket

Insulation

(5) Flue

Reset
button

(3) Thermostat

Gas
cock

(4) Gas
burner

Control
box

Thermocouple

Pilot
gas
tube

Burner
gas tube

How a gas water heater works: Hot water leaves tank through the **hot water outlet (1)** as fresh, cold water enters the water heater through the **dip tube (2)**. As the water temperature drops, the **thermostat (3)** opens the gas valve, and the **gas burner (4)** is lighted by pilot flame. Exhaust gases are vented through **flue (5)**. When water temperature reaches pre-set temperature, the thermostat closes gas valve, extinguishing burner. The thermocouple protects against gas leaks by automatically shutting off gas if pilot flame goes out. Anode rod protects tank lining from rust by attracting corrosive elements in the water. Pressure-relief valve guards against ruptures caused by steam buildup in tank.

Fixing a Water Heater

Standard tank water heaters are designed so that repairs are simple. All water heaters have convenient access panels that make it easy to replace worn-out parts. When buying new water heater parts, make sure the replacements match the specifications of your water heater. Most water heaters have a nameplate (page 274) that lists the information needed, including the pressure rating of the tank and the voltage and wattage ratings of the electric heating elements.

Many water heater problems can be avoided with routine yearly maintenance. Flush the water heater and test the pressure-relief valve once a year. Set the thermostat at a lower water temperature to prevent heat damage to the tank. (NOTE: Water temperature may affect the efficiency of automatic dishwashers. Check manufacturer's directions for recommended water temperature.) Water heaters last about 10 years on average, but with regular maintenance, a water heater can last 20 years or more.

Do not install an insulating jacket around a gas water heater. Insulation can block air supply and prevent the water heater from ventilating properly. Many water heater manufacturers prohibit the use of insulating jackets. To save energy, insulate the hot water pipes instead, using the materials described on page 292.

The pressure-relief valve is an important safety device that should be checked at least once each year and replaced, if needed. When replacing the pressure-relief valve, shut off the water and drain several gallons of water from the tank.

Problems		Repairs
	No hot water, or not enough hot water.	1. **Gas heater**: Make sure gas is on, then relight pilot flame (page 279). **Electric heater**: Make sure power is on, then reset thermostat (page 281). 2. Flush water heater to remove sediment in tank (photo, below). 3. Insulate hot water pipes to reduce heat loss (page 292). 4. **Gas heater**: Clean gas burner & replace thermocouple (pages 270 to 271). **Electric heater**: Replace heating element or thermostat (pages 272 to 273). 5. Raise temperature setting of thermostat.
	Pressure-relief valve leaks.	1. Lower the temperature setting (photo, below). 2. Install a new pressure-relief valve (pages 276 to 277, steps 10 to 11). 3. Install a water hammer arrester (page 295).
	Pilot flame will not stay lighted.	Clean gas burner & replace the thermocouple (pages 270 to 271).
	Water heater leaks around base of tank.	Replace the water heater immediately (pages 274 to 285).

Tips for Maintaining a Water Heater

Flush the water heater once a year by draining several gallons of water from the tank. Flushing removes sediment buildup that causes corrosion and reduces heating efficiency.

Lower the temperature setting on thermostat to 120° F. Lower temperature setting reduces damage to tank caused by overheating and also reduces energy use.

Fixing a Gas Water Heater

If a gas water heater does not heat water, first remove the outer and inner access panels and make sure the pilot is lighted. To relight a pilot, see steps 20 to 23, page 279. During operation, the outer and inner access panels must be in place. Operating the water heater without the access panels may allow air drafts to blow out the pilot flame.

If the pilot will not light, it is probably because the thermocouple is worn out. The thermocouple is a safety device designed to shut off the gas automatically if the pilot flame goes out. The thermocouple is a thin copper wire that runs from the control box to the gas burner. New thermocouples are inexpensive and can be installed in a few minutes.

If the gas burner does not light, even though the pilot flame is working, or if the gas burns with a yellow, smoky flame, the burner and the pilot gas tube should be cleaned. Clean the burner and gas tube annually to improve energy efficiency and extend the life of the water heater.

A gas water heater must be well ventilated. If you smell smoke or fumes coming from a water heater, shut off the water heater and make sure the exhaust duct is not clogged with soot. A rusted duct must be replaced.

Remember to shut off the gas before beginning work.

Everything You Need

Tools: adjustable wrench, vacuum cleaner, needlenose pliers.

Materials: thin wires, replacement thermocouple.

How to Clean a Gas Burner & Replace a Thermocouple

1 Shut off gas by turning the gas cock on top of the control box to the OFF position. Wait 10 minutes for gas to dissipate.

2 Disconnect the pilot gas tube, the burner gas tube, and the thermocouple from the bottom of the control box, using an adjustable wrench.

3 Remove the outer and inner access panels covering the burner chamber.

4 Pull down slightly on the pilot gas tube, the burner gas tube, and thermocouple wire to free them from the control box. Tilt the burner unit slightly and remove it from the burner chamber.

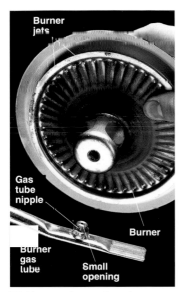

Burner jets

Gas tube nipple

Burner gas tube

Burner

Small opening

5 Unscrew burner from burner gas tube nipple. Clean small opening in nipple, using a piece of thin wire. Vacuum out burner jets and the burner chamber.

Pilot gas tube

6 Clean the pilot gas tube with a piece of wire. Vacuum out any loose particles. Screw burner onto gas tube nipple.

Thermocouple bracket

Thermocouple tip

7 Pull the old thermocouple from bracket. Install new thermo-couple by pushing the tip into the bracket until it snaps into place.

Mounting bracket

Tab

8 Insert the burner unit into the chamber. Flat tab at end of burner should fit into slotted open-ing in mounting bracket at the bottom of the chamber.

Burner gas tube

Pilot gas tube

Thermocouple

9 Reconnect the gas tubes and the thermocouple to the control box. Turn on the gas and test for leaks (page 278, step 19). Light the pilot (page 279, steps 20 to 23).

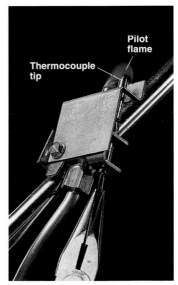

Thermocouple tip

Pilot flame

10 Make sure pilot flame wraps around tip of thermocouple. If needed, adjust thermocouple with needlenose pliers until tip is in flame. Replace the inner and outer access panels.

Electric water heater has one or two heating elements mounted in the side wall of the heater. Each element is connected to its own thermostat. When buying a replacement heating element or thermostat, make sure the replacement has same voltage and wattage rating as old part. This information is found on the nameplate (page 274).

Fixing an Electric Water Heater

The most common problem with an electric water heater is a burned-out heating element. Many electric water heaters have two heating elements. To determine which element has failed, turn on a hot water faucet and test the temperature. If the water heater produces water that is warm, but not hot, replace the top heating element. If the heater produces a small amount of very hot water, followed by cold water, replace the bottom heating element.

If replacing the heating element does not solve the problem, then the thermostat may have to be replaced. These parts are found under convenient access panels on the side of the heater.

Remember to turn off the power and test for current before touching wires (page 280, step 4).

Everything You Need

Tools: screwdriver, gloves, neon circuit tester, channel-type pliers.

Materials: masking tape, replacement heating element or thermostat, replacement gasket, pipe joint compound.

How to Replace an Electric Thermostat

1 Turn off power at main service panel. Remove access panel on side of heater, and **test for current (page 280, step 4).**

2 Disconnect thermostat wires, and label connections with masking tape. Pull old thermostat out of mounting clips. Snap new thermostat into place, and reconnect wires.

3 Press thermostat reset button, then use a screwdriver to set thermostat to desired temperature. Replace insulation and access panel. Turn on power.

1 Remove access panel on side of water heater. Shut off power to water heater (page 280, step 1). Close the shutoff valves, then drain tank (page 275, step 3).

2 Wearing protective gloves, carefully move insulation aside. **Caution:** Test for current (page 280, step 4), then disconnect wires on heating element. Remove protective collar.

3 Unscrew the heating element with channel-type pliers. Remove old gasket from around water heater opening. Coat both sides of new gasket with pipe joint compound.

4 Slide new gasket over heating element, and screw element into the tank. Tighten element with channel-type pliers.

5 Replace protective collar, and reconnect all wires. Turn on hot water faucets throughout house, then turn on water heater shutoff valves. When tap water runs steadily, close faucets.

6 Use a screwdriver to set thermostat to desired temperature. Press thermostat reset buttons. Fold insulation over thermostat, and replace the access panel. Turn on power.

Replacing a Water Heater

A water heater that leaks should be replaced immediately to prevent expensive water damage. Leaks occur because the inner tank has rusted through.

When replacing an electric water heater, make sure the voltage of the new model is the same as the old heater. When replacing a gas water heater, maintain a clearance of 6" or more around the unit for ventilation. Water heaters are available with tank sizes ranging from 30 to 65 gallons. A 40- or 50-gallon heater should be large enough for a family of four.

Energy-efficient water heaters have polyurethane foam insulation and usually carry an extended warranty. These models are more expensive, but over the life of the water heater they cost less to own and operate. Tankless water heaters are available and are a good replacement option (page 282).

The pressure-relief valve usually must be purchased separately. Make sure the new valve matches the *working pressure* rating of the tank (photo, left).

Everything You Need

Tools: pipe wrenches, hacksaw or tubing cutter, screwdriver, hammer, appliance dolly, level, small wire brush, propane torch, adjustable wrench, circuit tester (electric heaters).

Materials: bucket, wood shims, #1 gauge ⅜" sheetmetal screws, pressure-relief valve, threaded male pipe adapters, solder, two heat-saver nipples, Teflon tape, flexible water connectors, ¾" copper pipe, pipe joint compound, sponge, masking tape.

Nameplate on side of water heater lists tank capacity, insulation R-value, and working pressure (pounds per square inch). More efficient water heaters have an insulation R-value of 7 or higher. Nameplate for an electric water heater includes the voltage and the wattage capacity of the heating elements and thermostats. Water heaters also have a yellow **energy guide label** (photo, top) that lists typical yearly operating costs. Estimates are based on national averages. Energy costs in your area may vary.

1 Shut off the gas by turning the handle of the in-line valve so it is perpendicular to gas line. Wait 10 minutes for gas to dissipate. Shut off the water supply at the shutoff valves (photo, below).

2 Disconnect gas line at the union fitting or at the flare fitting below shutoff valve, using pipe wrenches. Disassemble and save the gas pipes and fittings.

3 Drain water from the water heater tank by opening the hose bib on the side of the tank. Drain the water into buckets, or attach a hose and empty the tank into a floor drain.

4 Disconnect the hot and cold water pipes above the water heater. If pipes are soldered copper, use a hacksaw or tubing cutter to cut through water pipes just below shutoff valves. Cuts must be straight.

5 Disconnect the exhaust duct by removing the sheetmetal screws. Remove the old water heater with an appliance dolly.

(continued next page)

6 Position new heater so that control box is close to gas line, and access panel for burner chamber is not obstructed.

7 Level the water heater by placing wood shims under the legs.

8 Position flue hat so legs fit into slots on water heater, then slip exhaust duct over flue hat. Make sure horizontal duct slopes upward ¼" per ft. so fumes cannot back up into house.

9 Attach the flue hat to the exhaust duct with #4 gauge ⅜" sheet-metal screws driven every 4".

10 Wrap threads of new pressure-relief valve with Teflon tape, and screw valve into tank opening with a pipe wrench.

11 Attach a copper or CPVC drain pipe to the pressure-relief valve, using threaded male adapter (page 43). Pipe should reach to within 3" of floor.

12 Solder threaded male adapters to the water pipes (pages 46 to 51). Let pipes cool, then wrap Teflon tape around threads of adapters.

13 Wrap Teflon tape around the threads of two heat-saver nipples. The nipples are color-coded, and have water-direction arrows to ensure proper installation.

14 Attach blue-coded nipple fitting to cold water inlet and red-coded fitting to hot water outlet, using a pipe wrench. On cold water nipple, water direction arrow should face down; on hot water nipple, arrow should face up.

15 Connect the water lines to the heat-saver nipples with flexible water connectors. Tighten fittings with an adjustable wrench.

(continued next page)

Union fitting

Nipple A

T-fitting

Nipple B

Nipple

Drip leg

Cap

16 Test-fit gas pipes and fittings from old water heater (step 2). One or two new black-iron nipples (A, B) may by necessary if new water heater is taller or shorter than old heater. Use black iron, not galvanized iron, for gas lines. Capped nipple is called a drip leg. The drip leg protects the gas burner by catching dirt particles.

17 Clean pipe threads with a small wire brush, and coat the threads with pipe joint compound. Assemble gas line in the following order: control box nipple (1), T-fitting (2), vertical nipple (3), union fitting (4), vertical nipple (5), cap (6). (Black iron is fitted using same methods as for galvanized iron. See pages 70 to 73 for more information.)

Flexible copper gas line

Flare nut

Alternate: If gas line is made of flexible copper, use a flare fitting to connect the gas line to the water heater. (For more information on flare fittings, see pages 54 to 55.)

18 Open the hot water faucets throughout house, then open the water heater inlet and outlet shutoff valves. When water runs steadily from faucets, close faucets.

19 Open the in-line valve on the gas line (step 1). Test for leaks by dabbing soapy water on each joint. Leaking gas will cause water to bubble. Tighten leaking joints with a pipe wrench.

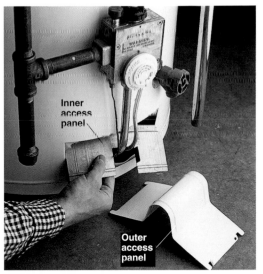

20 Turn the gas cock on top of control box to the PILOT position. Set the temperature control on front of box to desired temperature.

21 Remove the outer and inner access panels covering the burner chamber.

22 Light a match and hold flame next to the end of the pilot gas tube inside the burner chamber. Be sure to keep your face away from the opening.

23 While holding match next to end of pilot gas tube, press the reset button on top of control box. When pilot flame lights, continue to hold reset button for one minute. Turn gas cock to ON position, and replace the inner and outer access panels.

How to Replace a 220/240-volt Electric Water Heater

1 Turn off power to water heater by switching off circuit breaker (or removing fuse) at main service panel. Drain water heater and disconnect water pipes (page 275, steps 3 and 4).

2 Remove one of the heating element access panels on the side of the water heater.

3 Wearing protective gloves, fold back the insulation to expose the thermostat. **Caution: Do not touch bare wires until they have been tested for current.**

4 Test for current by touching probes of neon circuit tester to top pair of terminal screws on the thermostat. If tester lights, wires are not safe to work on; turn off main power switch and retest for current.

5 Remove coverplate on electrical box, found at side or top of water heater. Disconnect all wires, and label with masking tape for reference. Loosen cable clamp. Remove wires by pulling them through clamp. Remove old heater, then position new heater.

6 Connect water pipes and pressure-relief valve, following directions for gas water heaters (pages 276 to 277, steps 10 to 15). Open hot water faucets throughout the house, and turn on water. When water runs steadily, turn off faucets.

7 Remove the electrical box coverplate on new water heater. Thread the circuit wires through the clamp. Thread circuit wires through the cable opening on the water heater, and attach clamp to water heater.

8 Connect the circuit wires to the water heater wires, using wire connectors.

9 Attach bare copper or green ground wire to ground screw. Replace coverplate.

10 Remove access panels on side of water heater (steps 2 to 3), and use a screwdriver to set thermostats to desired water temperature.

11 Press reset button on thermostats. Replace the insulation and access panels. Turn on power.

Installing a Tankless Water Heater

A traditional tank water heater is no longer the only option for hot water supply. Tankless water heaters offer many advantages, including increased energy efficiency and a potentially unending supply of hot water. This is why they have been popular in Europe for a long time and are increasingly common in North America. Fueled by electricity, natural gas, or propane, a tankless heater works a bit like an automotive radiator: cold water enters the heater and flows through a matrix of coils, exiting the heater at temperatures from 100 to 140° F (default temperature on most models is 122° F).

A moderate-size tankless water heater will deliver 4 to 6 gallons of heated water per minute— enough volume to supply a shower or bathtub and a sink faucet or two. If your home has multiple bathrooms that are used concurrently, you can install a tankless heater with a higher output rate, such as 10 gallons per minute. But it may also make more sense for you to install multiple water heaters to supply various fixture and appliance "zones" in your home.

Gas-fueled tankless water heaters must be independently vented out of the house with 3-in. stainless steel vent pipe (gas rated). In many cases, you're required to install them in a twin-pipe system, where fresh air is piped directly into a sealed burner from outdoors.

From an efficiency and cost-of-operation standpoint, gas-fueled (either natural gas or liquid propane) burners make a great deal of sense. But installing one yourself is an extremely challenging and potentially dangerous DIY task. In fact, many plumbing contractors still refuse this installation work. Electric tankless heaters are a bit less risky to install and involve fewer considerations, such as meeting minimum supply pipe diameters. But this is still a task that's best left to a very experienced DIYer or a professional installer. A permit and on-site inspection are required.

NOTE: The following information is not intended to be comprehensive. Before installing a tankless water heater, the installer should read the installation manual completely and discuss the plan with local plumbing and wiring inspectors.

Everything You Need

Tools: pipe wrenches, hacksaw or tubing cutter, small wire brush, propane torch, adjustable wrench.

Materials: tankless water heater, ¾" copper pipe, exhaust pipe, gas supply pipe.

Inspect the rating plate (usually found on the cover of the heater) to make sure that the tankless heater is compatible with your fuel source. Units designed for liquid propane gas cannot be interchanged with units that burn natural gas.

Exhaust vent

Heat exchanger

Burners

Natural gas supply

Pressure relief valve

Hot water supply out

Cold water supply in

Gas-fueled tankless water heaters are very efficient, but they are also more difficult to install and may require that you replace gas supply pipes from the meter.

How to Install a Tankless Water Heater

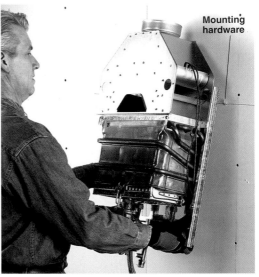

1 Attach the mounting hardware to the framing members as recommended. Make sure the unit will be level and positioned so the heater unit meets minimum clearance requirements.

2 Set the heater unit onto the mounting hardware. Run code-approved vent pipe from the unit out of the house. Follow local code regarding length of the vent and placement of the termination.

3 Attach the exhaust connector and gasket at the exhaust vent outlet. Insert the vent pipe into the connector. Install a condensate tube or trap in the exhaust line if required by code.

4 Run gas supply line from the main and connect to the unit as directed. Be absolutely certain that the pipe material and size meet minimum standards for the unit (flexible copper lines generally are not allowed and black iron pipe is preferred for natural gas). Also make sure the line is equipped with a manual shutoff valve near the heater unit.

5 Run cold water supply to the water inlet port on the heater unit and connect as directed. Insert an inlet filter screen between the supply line and the inlet port. Make certain that you are hooking the supply to the correct port.

6 Connect a pressure relief valve (PRV) to the hot supply line, making certain any shutoff valves are downstream from the PRV. Connect the hot water outlet to the correct outlet port with a compression fitting. Attach a discharge line to the PRV if required by code.

7 Follow manufacturer's instructions to make the electrical connections to operate the blower fan and the control panel. Most heater units must be independently grounded, as well.

8 Have the tankless water heater inspected before use. This will likely include leak and pressure inspections on the gas and water lines. Test the gas line for leaks by brushing soap suds onto the connection. Leaking gas will cause the suds to bubble up. Follow the manufacturer's instructions for setting up, operating, and maintaining your new tankless water heater.

Front View

Control panel

Drain hose

Timer

Access panel

Door gasket

Back View

Insulation

Drain hose

Fill tube

Pump assembly

Water inlet valve

A standard dishwasher is a slide-in appliance that can be pulled out from the cabinet when repairs are necessary.

Fixing a Dishwasher

Dishwashers are durable, low-maintenance appliances. The few problems that do occur can be solved relatively easily.

Replace a defective door gasket to eliminate leaks. If the gasket appears to be in good condition, adjust the door catch: loosen the retaining screws on the door catch, reposition it, and tighten the screws.

Replace a damaged or kinked drain hose to allow the unit to drain properly. Relocate water or waste lines that rest against the dishwasher to reduce excessive noise levels.

Clogged water lines can present more serious problems. A clogged screen or defective solenoid can keep the dishwasher from filling correctly. You can clean the inlet valve, which may solve the problem, but solenoid repair requires professional attention.

Everything You Need

Tools: pliers, screwdriver, continuity tester.

Materials: replacement drain hose, clamps, replacement gasket, replacement valve screen.

How to Replace a Drain Hose

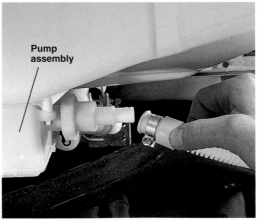

Pump assembly

Turn off power and water supply. Remove lower panel of unit, held in place by clips or screws. Place a baking pan or bowl under pump to catch any water trapped in drain hose. Loosen hose clamp with pliers or a screwdriver. Remove hose from pump. Detach other end of hose from drain or garbage disposer beneath sink. Install new hose, using new clamps. Restore power and water supply. Test unit to make sure it drains properly and there are no leaks in new hose.

How to Replace a Door Gasket

Inspect the gasket around the door. If it is cracked or damaged, replace it with a new one. Disconnect the electrical power at the main service panel. Pull out the bottom dish rack. Remove the old gasket, using a screwdriver to pry up the tabs or loosen the retaining screws that hold it in place. Soak the new gasket in warm soapy water to make it more pliable and to lubricate it. Install the new gasket by pressing or sliding it into its track. If the gasket has screws or clips, refasten as you go. Work from the center of the door to the ends.

How to Test an Inlet Valve & Replace the Valve Screen

Filler tube
Inlet valve
Water supply tube

Mounting bracket
Water inlet valve
Water supply port

1 Turn off power and water supply. Remove access panel and locate water supply connection. Disconnect wires from the terminals on inlet valve. Attach clip of a continuity tester to one terminal and touch probe to the other. If tester does not glow, solenoid is faulty and should be replaced. To replace the screen, place a shallow pan beneath valve. Release clamp and pull fill tube from valve outlet.

2 Disconnect the water supply tube. Loosen the valve bracket screws and remove valve. Remove the screen, using a small screwdriver. Replace screen with a new one and reinstall valve.

Water outlet

Control valve

Timer

Water inlet

Brine line

Drain line

Control unit

Resin tank | Float | Brine well | Brine tank

Drain line

A water softener includes two tanks: a resin tank (left) and a brine tank (right). Inside the brine tank is the brine well and float (center).

Maintaining a Water Softener

A water softener lowers the content of "hard" minerals in water—magnesium and calcium—and replaces them with sodium or potassium to help prolong the life of pipes and appliances.

A water softener has just a few mechanical parts—valves to control water flow in and out of the tank, and a timer, which regulates the recharging of the mineral tank by the brine tank.

If your water becomes hard, the brine tank may just need additional salt or potassium pellets. Because household demands vary, check your supply every week to determine how often the salt or potassium supply should be replenished (typically every couple of months).

An improperly set timer can cause hard water. Adjust it to run more frequently to ensure a constant supply of soft water. Iron content also causes hard water. Measure the iron content of your water supply occasionally, or add a water filter (pages 164 to 165) to help reduce the iron flow into the water softener.

Repair problems generally arise in the brine line or the control unit. Inspect the brine line every two years for buildup of sediment from the water supply or foreign particles in the salt or potassium. If the control unit needs servicing, remove it and bring it to your nearest dealer. Follow the removal instructions in the owner's manual for your particular unit.

Everything You Need

Tools: needlenose pliers, screwdriver, kitchen baster.

How to Inspect & Clean Brine Connections

1 Unplug softener. Divert the water supply by turning the bypass valve, or closing the inlet valve and turning on the nearest faucet. Turn timer dial to backwash. With a needlenose pliers, remove the compression nut connecting the brine line to the control unit. Inspect line for obstructions.

2 Remove particles or residue from the line, using a small screwdriver. Flush line with warm water—a funnel or kitchen baster is useful for this task—then reattach the brine line.

3 Inspect the brine injector. Do not reconnect power or make any changes to the supply or control dial. To gain access to the brine injector, which is often directly below the brine line connection, use a screwdriver to remove the cover. Unscrew injector from housing.

4 Pull off the injector filter screen covering the injector. Wash it with soap and water. Blow into injector or wipe it out with a soft cloth to clean. Do not use a sharp object that might scratch the metal and damage the injector. Reattach screen and screw injector back into place. Attach the cover. Return bypass valve to original position, or open inlet valve and turn off faucet. Reset the control dial and plug in softener.

Tighten or loosen the adjusting nut in small increments to increase or decrease the pressure in the tank.

A waterlogged tank can be fixed by shutting the supply valve, opening the drain valve, and running cold water in the house while the tank fills with air.

Maintaining a Water Pump

Well water systems use a pump to extract water from the underground aquifer, sending it up through the well pipe and depositing it into a galvanized steel water tank. As the tank fills, air pressure inside the tank increases until it trips a pressure switch, turning off the pump. The compressed air in the tank provides the pressure to supply the faucets. As water is drawn from the tank, the air pressure drops until the pressure gauge restarts the pump.

Two types of pumps are used in most residential wells: the submersible pump and the jet pump. Submersible pumps require less maintenance, with motors that can operate trouble-free for more than 20 years, but repair or replacement requires a truck-mounted derrick. Jet pumps are typically used with shallow wells or wells used seasonally, such as at summer cabins.

If low pressure problems occur in your well system, try adjusting the pressure setting on the pump. The maximum pressure rating should be listed near the gauge, but it may also be in the owner's manual. Contact the manufacturer if you can't locate the maximum ratings for your pump.

If the maximum setting is higher than the current setting, turn off power to the pump and remove the cover on the pressure switch to access the adjusting nut on the tall spring (illustration, top left).

Turn the nut clockwise to raise the pressure incrementally—1½ turns raises the pressure about 3 pounds. Cover the pressure switch and turn on the power. Watch the gauge as the pump runs through an entire cycle to make sure your adjustments have not increased the pressure above the maximum rating.

If the pump starts and stops frequently, the tank may be waterlogged. It must be drained and allowed to fill with air passively. First, close the supply valve between the pump and the water tank (illustration, bottom left). Turn on a cold-water faucet in the house to prevent a vacuum in the piping system.

Open the drain valve near the tank to allow the tank to drain completely. Wait a few minutes, then turn off the faucet and close the drain valve. Open the valve between the pump and the tank. As the tank fills, water will pressurize the air cushion. If this doesn't solve the problem, the pressure switch or air volume control may have to be serviced by an expert.

Have your tank inspected and emptied regularly.	A neglected tank will cause your system to fail, resulting in sewage backup and posing a serious risk to your family's health.
	Experts recommend pumping a septic tank every one to two years.
Avoid using chemicals.	Harsh chemicals and antibacterial agents kill the bacteria your system depends on.

	Keep these chemicals out of your toilets and house drains:
	    Drain cleaner
	    Paint and paint thinner
	    Chemical cleaners
	    Chlorine – including toilet bowl flush-cleaners
	    Antibacterial soft-soaps

Limit kitchen wastes.	Grease and fat from food hinder the septic process by coating drain pipes, interfering with bacterial breakdown in the tank, and clogging the loose-fill material in the drain field.
	Food disposers overload your system with solid food particles, sometimes doubling the rate of sludge accumulation in the tank.
	Throw cooking grease and food scraps in the garbage or compost heap.

Limit water inflow.
   Repair leaky plumbing fixtures as soon as possible.
   Route roof drains out of the house drain system.
   Don't drain a swimming pool or hot tub into the
     house drain.
	Excess water speeds up the flow through the septic system. The natural bacteria can't do their job, allowing too many solids to pass into the drain field.

Never use additives.	Biological additives designed to stimulate bacterial growth often harm more than they help. These additives agitate the anaerobic bacteria in the septic tank, and the increased activity forces undissolved solids into the drain field.

Maintaining a Septic System

Once problems arise within a septic system, there isn't much a homeowner can do. However, being able to identify early signs of trouble may prolong the life of your system and save you money.

If drains work slowly, or not at all, there may be a clog in the main house drain, or the septic system may be backed up. Check for clogs first. Clear the main drain with a motorized auger. Never use chemical drain cleaners.

If the house drain isn't clogged, the problem may be a clogged drain field, an absence of bacteria in the system, or a full septic tank. Common trouble signs also include dark-colored water on the surface of the drain field and a sewage odor in or around the home.

Any of these symptoms may indicate a serious problem. Human sewage is a hazardous waste, and strict regulations govern its removal. Septic tanks produce explosive methane gas and may contain deadly viruses. Contact a licensed sewer cleaning service to have the system inspected and serviced.

Septic tank

A properly maintained septic system feeds waste water into pipes that fan out into the drainage field. The remaining solid waste settles in the tank, and must be pumped out every few years for disposal.

Fixing Burst or Frozen Pipes

When a pipe bursts, immediately turn off the water at the main shutoff valve. Make temporary repairs with a sleeve clamp repair kit (page opposite).

A burst pipe is usually caused by freezing water. Prevent freezes by insulating pipes that run in crawl spaces or other unheated areas.

Pipes that freeze, but do not burst, will block water flow to faucets or appliances. Frozen pipes are easily thawed, but determining the exact location of the blockage may be difficult. Leave blocked faucets or valves turned on. Trace supply pipes that lead to blocked faucet or valve, and look for places where the line runs close to exterior walls or unheated areas. Thaw pipes with a heat gun or hair dryer (below).

Old fittings or corroded pipe also may leak or rupture. Fix old pipes according to the guidelines described on pages 44 to 77.

Begin any emergency repair by turning off water supply at main shutoff valve. The main shutoff valve is usually located near water meter.

Everything You Need
Tools: heat gun or hair dryer, gloves, metal file, screwdriver.
Materials: pipe insulation, sleeve clamp repair kit.

How to Repair Pipes Blocked with Ice

1 Thaw pipes with a heat gun or hair dryer. Use heat gun on low setting, and keep nozzle moving to prevent overheating pipes.

2 Let pipes cool, then insulate with sleeve-type foam insulation to prevent freezing. Use pipe insulation in crawl spaces or other unheated areas.

Alternate: Insulate pipes with fiberglass strip insulation and waterproof wrap. Wrap insulating strips loosely for best protection.

How to Temporarily Fix a Burst Pipe

1 Turn off water at main shutoff valve. Heat pipe gently with heat gun or hair dryer. Keep nozzle moving. Once frozen area is thawed, allow pipe to drain.

2 Smooth rough edges of rupture with metal file.

3 Place rubber sleeve of repair clamp around rupture. Make sure seam of sleeve is on opposite side of pipe from rupture.

4 Place the two metal repair clamps around rubber sleeve.

5 Tighten screws with screwdriver. Open water supply and watch for leaks. If repair clamp leaks, retighten screws. **Caution: Repairs made with a repair clamp kit are temporary.** Replace ruptured section of pipe as soon as possible.

Quieting Noisy Pipes

Pipes can make a loud banging noise when faucets are turned off or when valves on washing machines (or other automatic appliances) shut abruptly. The sudden stop of flowing water traps air and creates a shock wave, called water hammer, that slams through the water supply system. Some pipes may knock against wall studs or joists, creating additional noise.

Water hammer can be more than an annoyance. The shockwave can cause damage and eventually failure in pipes and fittings. If a pressure-relief valve on your water heater leaks (see page 269), it may not be a faulty valve, but a pressure surge in the supply system.

You can eliminate water hammer by installing a simple device called a water hammer arrester (see page 27) in the supply line. Inexpensive point-of-use arresters are small enough to be installed easily near the noisy valve or appliance (the closer the better). They can be positioned horizontally or vertically or at an angle without any change in effectiveness. Unlike with old-style air chambers, water cannot fill a water hammer arrester, so they should be effective for the life of the system.

Pipes that bang against studs or joists can be quieted by cushioning them with pieces of pipe insulation. Make sure pipe hangers are snug and that pipes are well supported.

Everything You Need

Tools: utility knife, reciprocating saw or hacksaw, propane torch (for sweating copper), pipe wrenches (for galvanized iron).

Materials: foam rubber pipe insulation, pipe and fittings, as needed.

Install cushions made from pieces of foam rubber pipe insulation to prevent pipes from banging against wall studs or joists.

Loose pipes may bang or rub against joist hangers, creating unwanted noises. Use pieces of foam rubber pipe insulation to cushion pipes.

1 Shut off water supply and drain pipes. Measure and cut out a section of horizontal pipe for T-fitting (pages 40 and 44 to 47).

2 Install a T-fitting as close to the valve as possible. Use techniques described on pages 48 to 50.

3 Install a short piece of pipe in the branch arm of the T-fitting. This short pipe will be used to attach a threaded fitting (step 4).

Short pipe

Branch arm

T-fitting

4 Install a threaded fitting. Use a fitting recommended by the manufacturer for your arrester.

5 Wrap the threads of the arrester in Teflon tape. Thread the arrester onto the fitting by hand. Tighten by holding the fitting with one adjustable wrench and turning the arrester with the other. Do not overtighten. Turn the water on and check for leaks.

Conversion Charts

Converting Measurements

To Convert:	To:	Multiply by:
Inches	Millimeters	25.4
Inches	Centimeters	2.54
Feet	Meters	0.305
Yards	Meters	0.914
Square inches	Square centimeters	6.45
Square feet	Square meters	0.093
Square yards	Square meters	0.836
Cubic inches	Cubic centimeters	16.4
Cubic feet	Cubic meters	0.0283
Cubic yards	Cubic meters	0.765
Ounces	Milliliters	30.0
Pints (U.S.)	Liters	0.473 (Imp. 0.568)
Quarts (U.S.)	Liters	0.946 (Imp. 1.136)
Gallons (U.S.)	Liters	3.785 (Imp. 4.546)
Ounces	Grams	28.4
Pounds	Kilograms	0.454

To Convert:	To:	Multiply by:
Millimeters	Inches	0.039
Centimeters	Inches	0.394
Meters	Feet	3.28
Meters	Yards	1.09
Square centimeters	Square inches	0.155
Square meters	Square feet	10.8
Square meters	Square yards	1.2
Cubic centimeters	Cubic inches	0.061
Cubic meters	Cubic feet	35.3
Cubic meters	Cubic yards	1.31
Milliliters	Ounces	.033
Liters	Pints (U.S.)	2.114 (Imp. 1.76)
Liters	Quarts (U.S.)	1.057 (Imp. 0.88)
Liters	Gallons (U.S.)	0.264 (Imp. 0.22)
Grams	Ounces	0.035
Kilograms	Pounds	2.2

Metric Equivalents

	1/64	1/32	1/25	1/16	1/8	1/4	3/8	2/5	1/2	5/8	3/4	7/8	1	2	3	4	5	6	7	8	9	10	11	12	36	39.4
Inches (in.)	1/64	1/32	1/25	1/16	1/8	1/4	3/8	2/5	1/2	5/8	3/4	7/8	1	2	3	4	5	6	7	8	9	10	11	12	36	39.4
Feet (ft.)																								1	3	3 1/12
Yards (yd.)																									1	1 1/12
Millimeters (mm)	0.40	0.79	1	1.59	3.18	6.35	9.53	10	12.7	15.9	19.1	22.2	25.4	50.8	76.2	101.6	127	152	178	203	229	254	279	305	914	1,000
Centimeters (cm)							0.95	1	1.27	1.59	1.91	2.22	2.54	5.08	7.62	10.16	12.7	15.2	17.8	20.3	22.9	25.4	27.9	30.5	91.4	100
Meters (m)																								.30	.91	1.00

Resources

National Kitchens & Bathroom Association
(NKBA)
800-843-6522
www.nkba.com

Plumbing and Drainage Institute
45 Bristol Drive
South Easton, MA 02375
www.pdionline.org

International Association of Plumbing and Mechanical Officials
20001 E. Walnut Drive South
Walnut, CA 91789-2825
www.iapmo.org

Plumbing Heating Cooling Information Bureau
222 Merchandise Mart Plaza
Chicago, IL 60654
www.phcib.org

The Institute of Plumbing
64 Station Lane, Hornchurch
Essex, RM12 6NM, England
www.worldplumbing.org

International Conference of Building Officials
5360 Workman Mill Rd.
Whittier, CA 90601-2298
800-284-4406

Kleve Heating & Air
13075 Pioneer trail
Eden Prairie, MN 55344

Photography Contributors

Delta Faucet Company
317-848-1812
www.deltafaucet.com
page 206

Fluidmaster, Inc. 2001
949-728-2000
www.fluidmaster.com
waxless toilet gasket inset
page 130

GROHE America, Inc.
630-582-7711
www.groheamerica.com
page 154

Hunter Industries
760-744-5240
www.hunterindustries.com
pages 175 and 179

In-Sink-Erator®
800-558-5700
www.insinkerator.com
page 162

OATEY
800-321-9532
www.oatey.com
pages 146 (top); 147 (top right)

SFA Saniflo, Inc.
800-363-5874
www.saniflo.com
pages 132-133 (all)

Whirlpool
800-253-1301
www.whirlpool.com
page 160

INDEX